THE
Classic Country
BOOK

D0521799

Cover guitar courtesy of Crown Music

ISBN 0-7935-5866-2

HAL•LEONARD®
CORPORATION
7777 W. BLUEMOUND RD. P.O. BOX 13819 MILWAUKEE, WI 53213

THE Classic Country BOOK

CONTENTS

4 Strum and Pick Patterns

6 Act Naturally - *Buck Owens*

8 Always on My Mind - *Willie Nelson*

11 Amanda - *Waylon Jennings*

9 (Hey, Won't You Play) Another Somebody Done Somebody Wrong Song - *B.J. Thomas*

14 Any Time - *Eddy Arnold*

18 Bouquet of Roses - *Eddy Arnold, Mickey Gilley*

5 Busted - *John Conlee, Johnny Cash*

12 By the Time I Get to Phoenix - *Glen Campbell*

17 Chug-A-Lug - *Roger Miller*

22 Cold, Cold Heart - *Hank Williams*

26 Could I Have This Dance - *Anne Murray*

20 Country Bumpkin - *Cal Smith*

23 Crazy - *Patsy Cline*

24 Crazy Arms - *Ray Price*

25 Crying My Heart Out Over You - *Ricky Skaggs*

28 Daddy Sang Bass - *Johnny Cash*

32 Dang Me - *Roger Miller*

30 Deeper than the Holler - *Randy Travis*

33 Detroit City - *Bobby Bare*

36 D-I-V-O-R-C-E - *Tammy Wynette*

38 Easy Loving - *Freddie Hart*

40 El Paso - *Marty Robbins*

34 Faded Love - *Willie Nelson & Ray Price, Patsy Cline, Bob Wills*

44 The Fightin' Side of Me - *Merle Haggard*

46 Flowers on the Wall - *Statler Brothers*

43 Folsom Prison Blues - *Johnny Cash*

48 (Now and Then There's) A Fool Such as I - *Hank Snow*

50 Funny How Time Slips Away - *Willie Nelson, Lyle Lovett & Al Green*

51 Funny Way of Laughin' - *Burl Ives*

52 The Gambler - *Kenny Rogers*

56 Gentle on My Mind - *Glen Campbell*

58 Golden Ring - *George Jones & Tammy Wynette*

15 Green Green Grass of Home - *Tom Jones, Porter Wagoner*

59 The Happiest Girl in the Whole U.S.A. - *Donna Fargo*

62 Have I Told You Lately That I Love You - *Kitty Wells & Red Foley, Gene Autrey*

63 He Stopped Loving Her Today - *George Jones*

64 Heartaches by the Number - *Guy Mitchell, Ray Price*

65 Hello Walls - *Faron Young*

66 Help Me Make It Through the Night - *Sammi Smith*

67 Hey, Good Lookin' - *Hank Williams*

68 Honky Tonk Blues - *Charley Pride, Hank Williams*

70 I Fall to Pieces - *Patsy Cline, A. Neville & Trisha Yearwood*

71 I Walk the Line - *Johnny Cash*

72 I'm Not Lisa - *Jessi Colter*

77 I'm So Lonesome I Could Cry - *Hank Williams*

74 If We Make It Through December - *Merle Haggard*

78 Islands in the Stream - *Kenny Rogers & Dolly Parton*

80 It Was Almost Like a Song - *Ronnie Milsap*

83 It's Not Love (But It's Not Bad) - *Merle Haggard*

82 Jambalaya (On the Bayou) - *Hank Williams*

86 King of the Road - *Roger Miller*

87 Kiss an Angel Good Mornin' - *Charley Pride*

84 The Last Word in Lonesome Is Me - *Eddy Arnold*

89 Leavin' on Your Mind - *Patsy Cline, Bobbie Roy*

92 Little Green Apples - *O.C. Smith, Roger Miller*

90 Living Proof - *Ricky Van Shelton*

95 The Long Black Veil - *Lefty Frizzell*

96 Lookin' for Love - *Johnny Lee*

98 Lucille - *Kenny Rogers*

101 Luckenbach, Texas (Back to the Basics of Love) - *Waylon Jennings & Willie Nelson*

104 Make the World Go Away - *Eddy Arnold*

105 Mama Tried - *Merle Haggard*

108 Mammas Don't Let Your Babies Grow Up to Be Cowboys - *Waylon Jennings & Willie Nelson, Gibson/Miller Band*

110 Mississippi Woman - *Waylon Jennings*

116 My Elusive Dreams - *David Houston & Tammy Wynette*

112 My Heroes Have Always Been Cowboys - *Willie Nelson*

114 Night Life - *Willie Nelson & Danny Davis, Ray Price*

117 Okie from Muskogee - *Merle Haggard*

120 Old Dogs, Children and Watermelon Wine - *Tom T. Hall*

118 Older Women - *Ronnie McDowell*

122 Paper Roses - *Anita Bryant, Marie Osmond*

124 Pick Me Up on Your Way Down - *Charlie Walker*

128 (I'm A) Ramblin' Man - *Waylon Jennings*

106 Rocky Top - *Lynn Anderson, Roger Whittaker*

127 Room Full of Roses - *Mickey Gilley*

130 Ruby, Don't Take Your Love to Town - *Kenny Rogers, Johnny Darrell*

132 Saginaw, Michigan - *Lefty Frizzell*

134 Satin Sheets - *Jeanne Pruett*

139 She Believes in Me - *Kenny Rogers*

125 She's Got You - *Patsy Cline, Loretta Lynn*

136 Sixteen Tons - *Tennessee Ernie Ford*

137 Some Days Are Diamonds (Some Days Are Stone) - *John Denver*

142 Son-of-a-Preacher Man - *Dusty Springfield*

144 (I'm A) Stand by My Woman Man - *Ronnie Milsap*

146 Streets of Bakersfield - *Dwight Yoakam & Buck Owens*

148 Sunday Mornin' Comin' Down - *Kris Kristofferson*

150 Tennessee Flat Top Box - *Johnny Cash, Roseanne Cash,*

152 The Vows Go Unbroken (Always True to You) - *Kenny Rogers*

155 Walking the Floor over You - *Ernest Tubb*

156 Waterloo - *Stonewall Jackson*

157 Welcome to My World - *Eddy Arnold*

159 Wheels - *Restless Heart*

158 When Two Worlds Collide - *Jerry Lee Lewis, Jim Reeves*

162 Why Me? (Why Me, Lord?) - *Kris Kristofferson, Cristy Lane*

174 Will the Circle Be Unbroken - *Johnny Cash*

164 You Decorated My Life - *Kenny Rogers*

166 You Don't Know Me - *Mickey Gilley, Eddy Arnold*

168 You Don't Want My Love - *Roger Miller*

170 You Needed Me - *Anne Murray*

172 You're the Reason God Made Oklahoma - *David Frizzell & Shelly West*

153 Your Cheatin' Heart - *Hank Williams, Patsy Cline*

STRUM AND PICK PATTERNS

This chart contains the suggested strum and pick patterns that are referred to by number at the beginning
of each song in this book. The symbols ⊓ and ∨ in the strum patterns refer to down and up strokes, respectively.
The letters in the pick patterns indicate which right-hand fingers plays which strings.

p = thumb
i = index finger
m = middle finger
a = ring finger

For example; Pick Pattern 2
is played: thumb - index - middle - ring

Strum Patterns

Pick Patterns

You can use the 3/4 Strum or Pick Patterns in songs written in compound meter (6/8, 9/8, 12/8, etc.).
For example, you can accompany a song in 6/8 by playing the 3/4 pattern twice in each measure.
The 4/4 Strum and Pick Patterns can be used for songs written in cut time (¢) by doubling the note
time values in the patterns. Each pattern would therefore last two measures in cut time.

Busted

Words and Music by Harlan Howard

Strum Pattern: 11
Pick Pattern: 8

Verse
Slow Blues

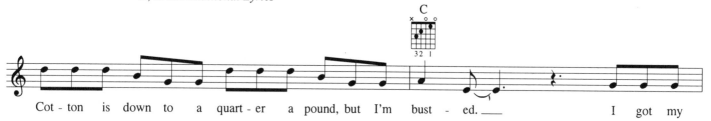

1. My bills are all due and the ba - by needs shoes and I'm bust - ed. ___
2., 3. *See Additional Lyrics*

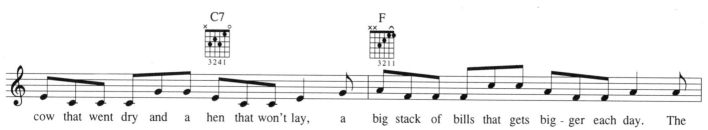

Cot - ton is down to a quart - er a pound, but I'm bust - ed. ___ I got my

cow that went dry and a hen that won't lay, a big stack of bills that gets big - ger each day. The

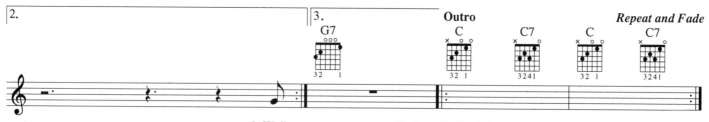

coun - ty's gon-na haul my be - long-ings a - way 'cause I'm bust - ed. ___   2. I

3. Well,   *Spoken: I'm broke! No bread! I mean like nothin'. Forget it!*

Additional Lyrics

2. I went to my brother to ask for a loan 'cause I was busted.
I hate to beg like a dog without his bone but I'm busted.
My brother said, "There ain't a thing I can do;
My wife and my kids are all down with the flu;
And I was just thinking about calling on you! And I'm busted."

3. Well, I am no thief but a man can go wrong when he's busted.
The food that we canned last summer is gone and I'm busted.
The fields are all bare and the cotton won't grow.
Me and my fam'ly got to pack up and go,
But I'll make a living, just where I don't know, 'cause I'm busted.

Act Naturally

Words and Music by Vonie Morrison and Johnny Russell

Strum Pattern: 3
Pick Pattern: 5

make me a big ___ star   'cause I can play the part so

Verse

well.   2., 4. Well, I hope you come and see me in the mov - ies.

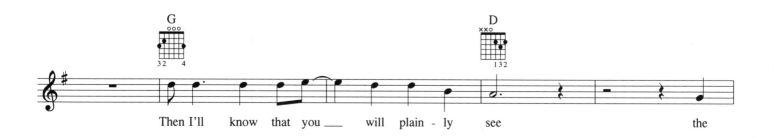

Then I'll know that you ___ will plain - ly see   the

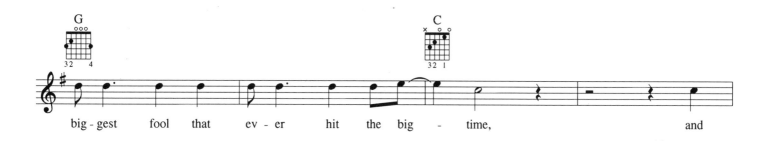

big - gest fool that ev - er hit the big - time,   and

all I got - ta do is act nat - 'ral - ly.

Outro

1.   2.

3. We'll

Additional Lyrics

3. We'll make the scene about a man that's sad and lonely,
   And beggin' down upon his bended knee.
   I'll play the part but I won't need rehearsin'.
   All I have to do is act nat'rally.

Always on My Mind

Words and Music by Wayne Thompson, Mark James and Johnny Christopher

Strum Pattern: 1
Pick Pattern: 2

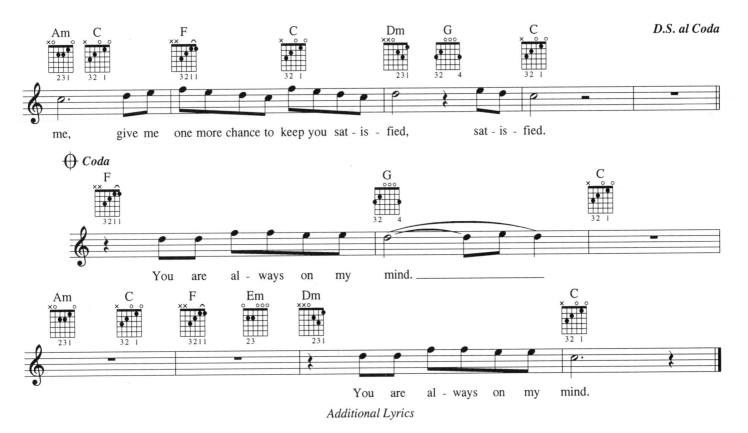

me, give me one more chance to keep you sat - is - fied, sat - is - fied.

Coda

You are al - ways on my mind. _____

You are al - ways on my mind.

Additional Lyrics

2. Maybe I didn't hold you all those lonely, lonely times,
And maybe I never told you I'm so happy that you're mine;
If I make you feel second best,
Girl I'm sorry I was blind.

(Hey, Won't You Play)
Another Somebody Done
Somebody Wrong Song

Words and Music by Larry Butler and Chips Moman

Strum Pattern: 2
Pick Pattern: 3

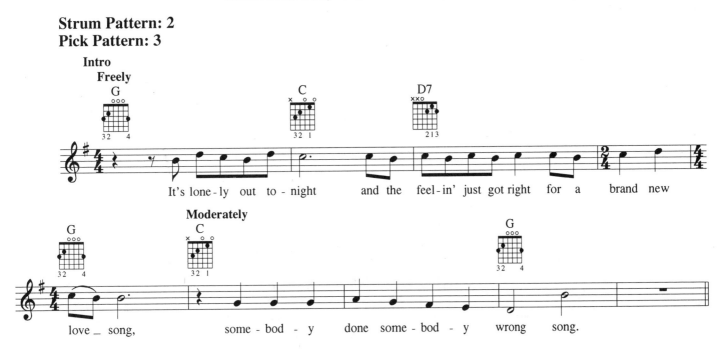

It's lone - ly out to - night and the feel - in' just got right for a brand new

love _ song, some - bod - y done some - bod - y wrong song.

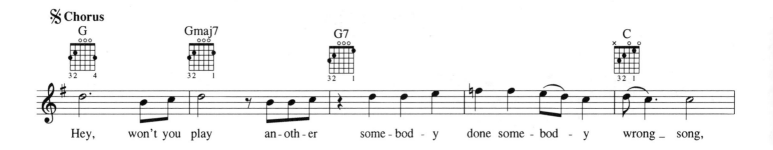

Hey, won't you play an-oth-er some-bod-y done some-bod-y wrong _ song,

To Coda ⊕

and make me feel at home _ while I miss my ba-by, while I miss my

Verse

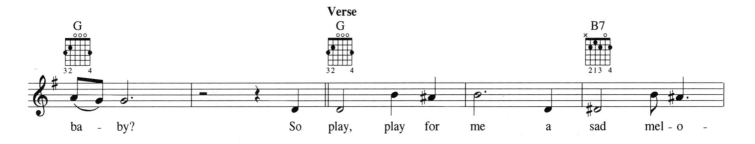

ba-by? So play, play for me a sad mel-o-

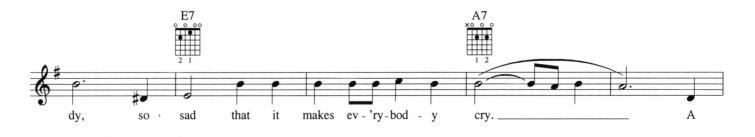

dy, so sad that it makes ev-'ry-bod-y cry. _____ A

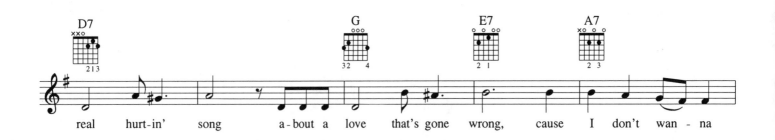

real hurt-in' song a-bout a love that's gone wrong, cause I don't wan-na

D.S. al Coda ⊕ *Coda*

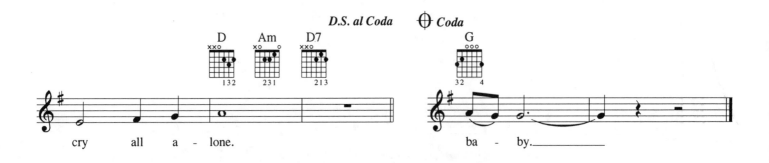

cry all a-lone.   baby. _____

Amanda

Words and Music by Bob McDill

Strum Pattern: 7
Pick Pattern: 9

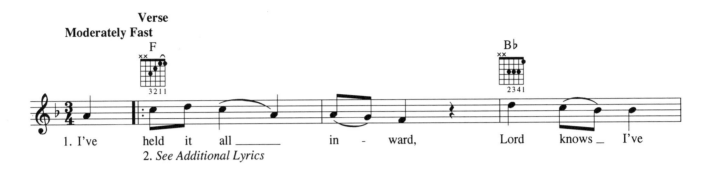

Verse
Moderately Fast

1. I've held it all _____ in - ward, Lord knows _ I've

2. *See Additional Lyrics*

tried. ___ It's an aw - ful ____ a - wak - 'ning' in a coun - try boy's _

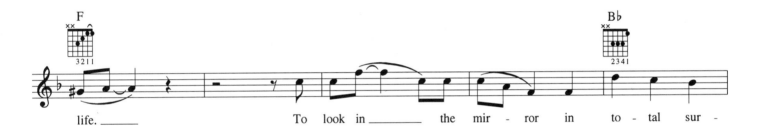

life. _____ To look in _____ the mir - ror in to - tal sur -

prise _____ at the hair on _____ your shoul - ders and the

Chorus

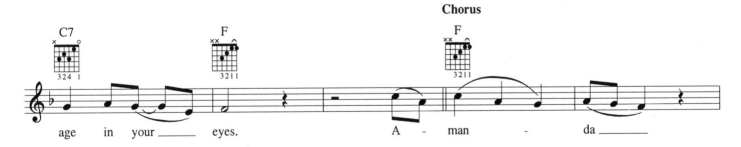

age in your ____ eyes. A - man - da _____

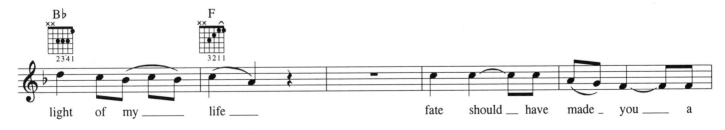

light of my ____ life _____ fate should _ have made _ you ____ a

gen - tle - man's wife. ___ A - man - da ___

light of my ___ life ___ fate should ___ have made _ you ___ a

gen - tle - man's wife. 2. Well the wife. _____

Additional Lyrics

2. Well the measure of people don't understand
   The pleasures of a life in a hillbilly band.
   I got my first guitar when I was fourteen.
   Now I'm crowding thirty and still wearin' jeans.

By the Time I Get to Phoenix

Words and Music by Jimmy Webb

Strum Pattern: 3
Pick Pattern: 3

1. By the time ___ I get to Phoe - nix ___ she'll be ris - in'. ___
2., 3. *See Additional Lyrics*

She'll find the note ___ I left hang-in' ___ on her door. She'll

Additional Lyrics

2. By the time I make Albuquerque she'll be workin'.
   She'll prob'ly stop at lunch and give me a call.
   But, she'll just hear that phone keep on ringin',
   Off the wall, that's all.

3. By the time I make Oklahoma she'll be sleepin'.
   She'll turn softly and call my name out low.
   And she'll cry just to think I'd really leave her,
   'Tho' time and time I've tried to tell her so.
   She just didn't know, I would really go.

Any Time

Words and Music by Herbert Happy Lawson

Strum Pattern:4
Pick Pattern:5

say   you   want   me   back   a   gain,   that's   the   time   I'll   come   back   home   to

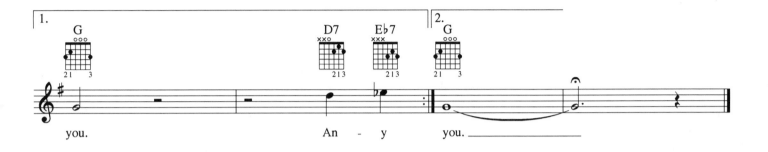

1.
you.   An - y

2.
you. _____

Green Green Grass of Home

Words and Music by Curly Putman

Strum Pattern: 2
Pick Pattern: 4

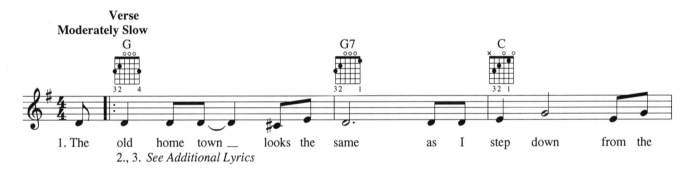

Verse
Moderately Slow

1. The   old   home   town ___   looks   the   same   as   I   step   down   from   the
2., 3. *See Additional Lyrics*

train, _____   and   there   to   meet   me   in   my   ma - ma _____   and   pa - pa. ___

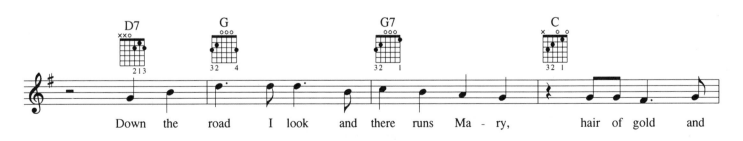

Down   the   road   I   look   and   there   runs   Ma - ry,   hair   of   gold   and

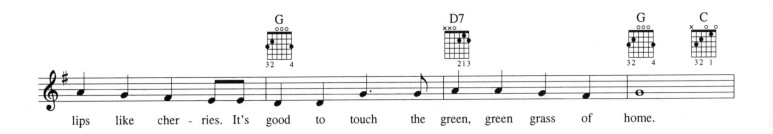

lips like cher - ries. It's good to touch the green, green grass of home.

Chorus

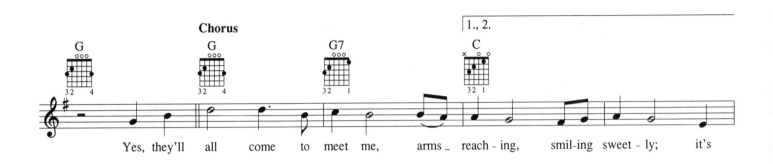

Yes, they'll all come to meet me, arms _ reach - ing, smil-ing sweet - ly; it's

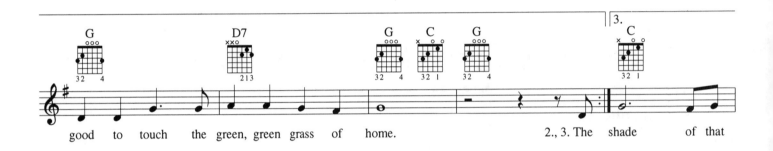

good to touch the green, green grass of home. 2., 3. The shade of that

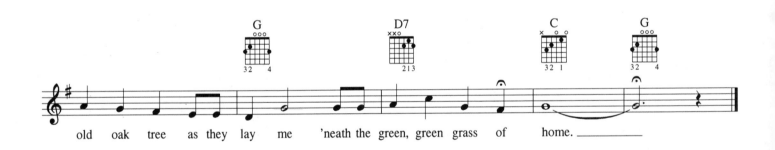

old oak tree as they lay me 'neath the green, green grass of home. _____

Additional Lyrics

2. The old house is still standing, though the paint is cracked and dry,
And there's that old oak tree that I used to play on.
Down the lane I walk with my sweet Mary,
Hair of gold and lips like cherries.
It's good to touch the green, green grass of home.

Chorus Yes, they'll all come to meet me,
Arms reaching, smiling sweetly;
It's good to touch the green, green grass of home.

3. (Spoken) Then I awake and look around me at four gray walls that surround me,
And I realize that I was only dreaming.
For there's a guard and there's a sad old padre.
Arm in arm, we'll walk at daybreak,
Again I'll touch the green, green grass of home.

Chorus Yes, they'll all come to see me,
In the shade of that old oak tree,
As they lay me 'neath the green, green grass of home.

Chug-A-Lug

Words and Music by Roger Miller

Strum Pattern: 3
Pick Pattern: 2

Verse
Moderately Fast

1. Grape wine in a ma-son jar, home-made and brought to school
2., 3. *See Additional Lyrics*

by a friend of mine af-ter class. Me and him and this oth-er fool de-

cide that we'll drink up what's left chug-a-lug; so we helped our-selves,

first time for ev-'ry-thing! Umm my ears still ring: Chug-a-lug, chug-a-

Chorus

lug _____ makes you want-a hol-ler hi-de-ho, burns _____ your tum-my

don't-cha know? Chug-a-lug, chug-a-lug! lug!

Additional Lyrics

2. 4-H and FFA on a field trip to the farm.
   Me and a friend sneak off behind,
   This big old barn where we uncovered a covered up moonshine still,
   And we thought we'd drink our fill.
   I swallered it with a smile; I run ten miles.

3. Jukebox and a sawdust floor, somethin' like I ain't seen before.
   And I'm just goin' on fifteen,
   But with the help of my faneglin' uncle I got snuck in,
   For my first taste of sin.
   I said, "Let me have a big ol' sip." I done a double back flip.

Bouquet of Roses

Words and Music by Steve Nelson and Bob Hilliard

Strum Pattern: 3
Pick Pattern: 3

Bridge

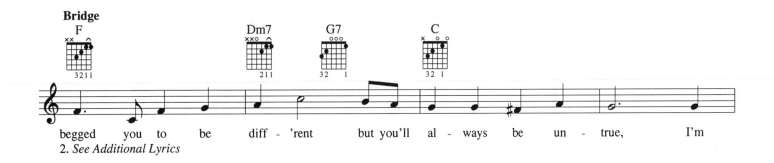

begged you to be diff-'rent but you'll al-ways be un-true, I'm

2. See Additional Lyrics

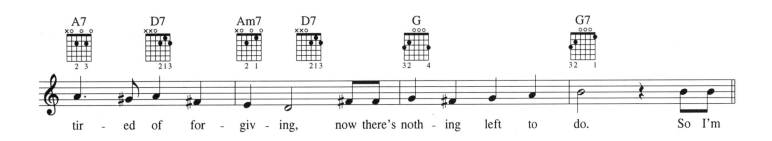

tir - ed of for - giv - ing, now there's noth - ing left to do. So I'm

Chorus

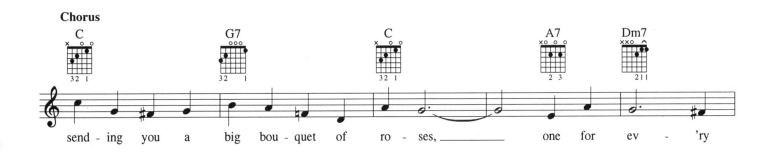

send - ing you a big bou - quet of ro - ses, _____ one for ev - 'ry

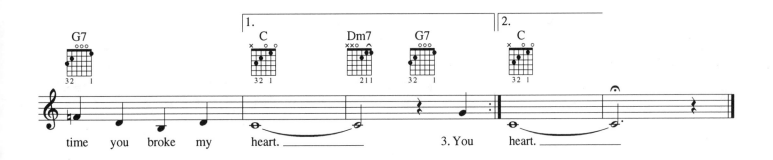

time you broke my heart. _____ 3. You heart. _____

Additional Lyrics

2. You made our lovers lane a road of sorrow,
   Till at last we had to say goodbye.
   You're leaving me to face each new tomorrow,
   With a broken heart you taught to cry.

Bridge I know that I should hate you after all you put me through,
        But how can I be bitter, when I'm still in love with you?

Country Bumpkin

Words and Music by Don Wayne

Strum Pattern: 1
Pick Pattern: 2

Intro
Moderately

1. He

Verse

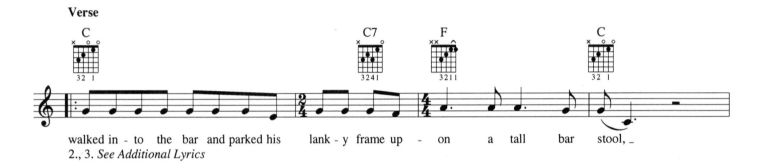

walked in - to the bar and parked his lank - y frame up - on a tall bar stool, _

2., 3. *See Additional Lyrics*

and with a long, soft south - ern drawl, said, "I'll have me a glass of an - y - thing that's

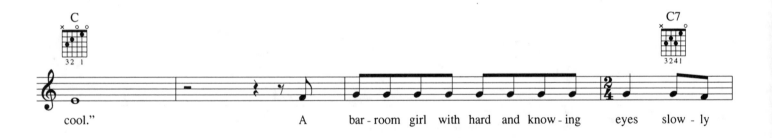

cool." A bar - room girl with hard and know - ing eyes slow - ly

looked him up _____ and down, _ and she thought, "I won - der how on earth that

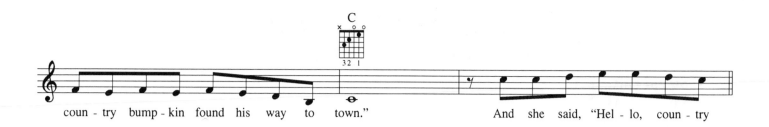

coun - try bump - kin found his way to town." And she said, "Hel - lo, coun - try

% Chorus

bump - kin, how's the frost out on the pump - kin? _____

I've seen some sights but, man, you're some - thin'. _____ Where'd you come from, coun - try

1., 2.　　　　　　　　　　　　　　3.

D.S. and Fade
(3rd Chorus)

bump - kin?"　　　　　　2. It was bump - kin."　　　And she said, "So long, coun - try

Additional Lyrics

2. It was just a short year later in a bed of joyfilled tears yet death-like pain,
   Into this wonderous world of many wonders one more wonder came.
   That same woman's face was wrapped in a raptured look of love and tenderness,
   As she marvelled at the soft and warm cuddly boy child feeding at her breast.

   Chorus And she said, "Hello country bumpkin, fresh as frost out on the pumpkin;
   I've seen some sights but, babe, you're somethin'! Mama loves her country bumpkin."

3. Forty years of hard work later, in a simple quiet and peaceful country place.
   The heavy hand of time had not erased the raptured wonder from the woman's face.
   She was lying on her deathbed knowing fully well her race was nearly won,
   But she softly smiled and looked into the sad eyes of her husband and son.

   Chorus And she said, "So long country bumpkin, the frost is gone now from the pumpkin.
   I've seen some sights and life's been somethin'. See you later, country bumpkin."
   And she said, "So long, country..."

Cold, Cold Heart

Words and Music by Hank Williams

Strum Pattern: 4
Pick Pattern: 5

Additional Lyrics

2. Another love before my time made your heart sad and blue,
   And so my heart is paying now for things I didn't do.
   In anger, unkind things are said that make the teardrops start.

3. You'll never know how much it hurts to see you sit and cry.
   You know you need and want my love yet you're afraid to try.
   Why do you run and hide from life? To try it just ain't smart.

4. There was a time when I believed that you belonged to me,
   But now I know your heart is shackled to a memory.
   The more I learn to care for you the more we drift apart.

Crazy

Words and Music by Willie Nelson

Strum Pattern: 4
Pick Pattern: 3

Crazy Arms

Words and Music by Ralph Mooney and Charles Seals

Strum Pattern: 2
Pick Pattern: 5

Verse
Moderately Fast

1. Blue ain't the word for the way that I feel. And a storm is brew-ing
2. *See Additional Lyrics*

in this heart of mine. _____ This is no trea-sured dream, I

know that it's real. You're some-one else's _ love now; you're not mine. _____

Chorus

Cra - zy arms that reach to hold som-bod-y new, but my yearn-ing heart keeps

say - ing you're not mine. _____ My trou-bled mind knows soon to an-oth-er you'll be

wed, and that's why I'm lone-ly all the time. _____

Additional Lyrics

2. Please take the treasured dreams I've had for you and me,
   And take all the love I thought was mine.
   Someday my crazy arms will hold someone new.
   But now I'm so lonely all the time.

Crying My Heart Out Over You

Words and Music by Carl Butler, Marijohn Wilkin, Louise Certain and Gladys Stacey

Strum Pattern: 2
Pick Pattern: 2

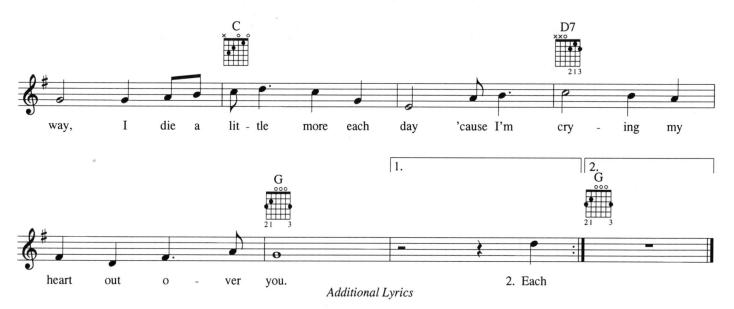

way, I die a lit-tle more each day 'cause I'm cry - ing my

heart out o - ver you.

Additional Lyrics

2. Each night I climb the stairs up to my room,
   It seems I hear you whisper in the gloom.
   I miss your picture on the wall, and your footsteps in the hall,
   While I'm crying my heart out over you.

Could I Have This Dance

Words and Music by Wayland Holyfield and Bob House

Strum Pattern: 9
Pick Pattern: 6

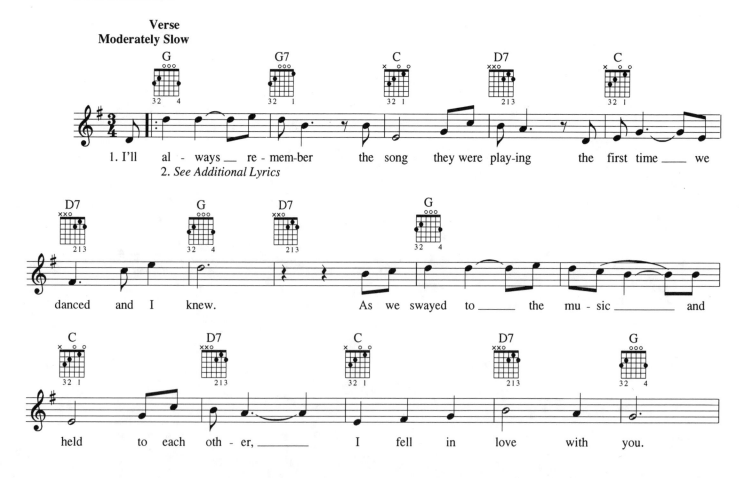

Verse
Moderately Slow

1. I'll al - ways __ re - mem - ber the song they were play-ing the first time __ we
2. *See Additional Lyrics*

danced and I knew. As we swayed to ____ the mu - sic _____ and

held to each oth - er, _____ I fell in love with you.

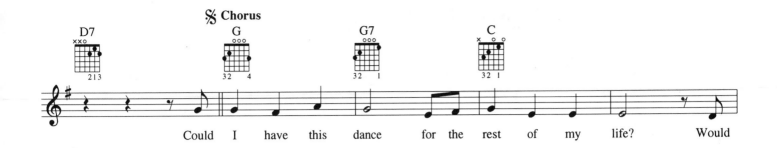

Could   I   have   this   dance   for   the   rest   of   my   life?   Would

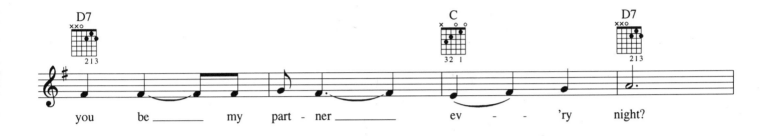

you   be _____ my   part - ner _____ ev - - 'ry   night?

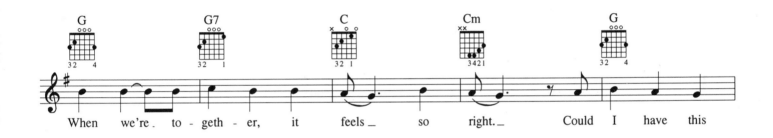

When   we're   to - geth - er,   it   feels __ so   right. __   Could   I   have   this

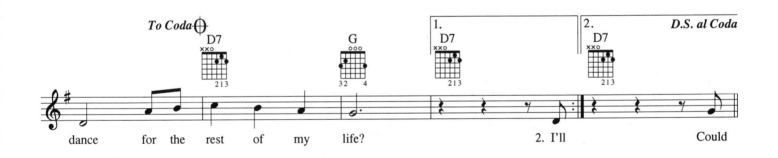

To Coda ⊕

dance   for   the   rest   of   my   life?   2. I'll   Could

D.S. al Coda

1.   2.

⊕ *Coda*

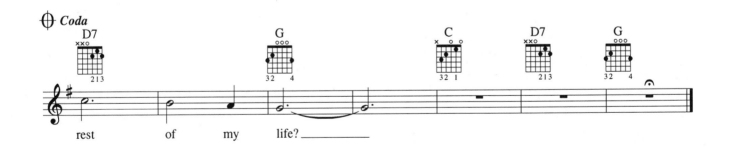

rest   of   my   life? _____

Additional Lyrics

2. I'll always remember that magic moment
When I held you close to me.
As we moved together, I knew forever
You're all I'll ever need.

Daddy Sang Bass

Words and Music by Carl Perkins

Strum Pattern: 4
Pick Pattern: 5

ten - or me and lit - tle bro-ther would join right in there sing - in' seems to

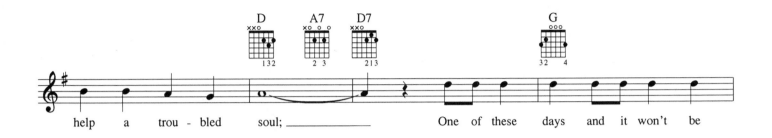

help a trou - bled soul; _____ One of these days and it won't be

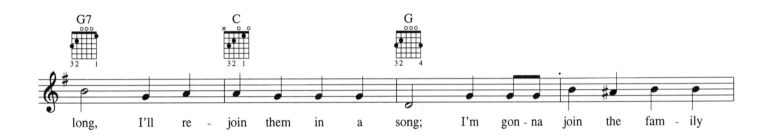

long, I'll re - join them in a song; I'm gon - na join the fam - ily

Bridge

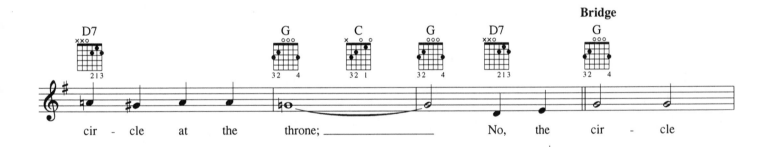

cir - cle at the throne; _____ No, the cir - cle

D.S. and Fade

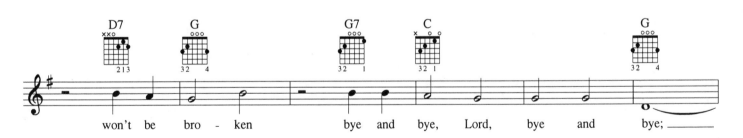

won't be bro - ken bye and bye, Lord, bye and bye; _____

Chorus

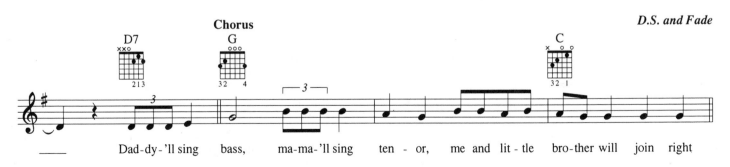

_____ Dad-dy-'ll sing bass, ma-ma-'ll sing ten - or, me and lit - tle bro-ther will join right

Deeper than the Holler

Words and Music by Don Schlitz and Paul Overstreet

Strum Pattern: 3
Pick Pattern: 4

MCA music publishing

Additional Lyrics

3. From the backroads to the Broadway shows
   With a million miles between,
   There's at least a million love songs
   That people love to sing.
   And ev'ryone is diff'rent,
   And everyone's the same.
   And this is just another way
   Of saying the same thing.

Dang Me

Words and Music by Roger Miller

Strum Pattern: 3
Pick Pattern: 2

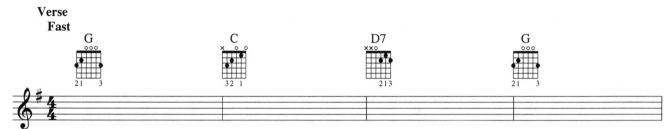

1. *Spoken:* Well, here I sit high gettin' ideas, ain't nothin' but a fool would live like this.
2., 3. *See Additional Lyrics*

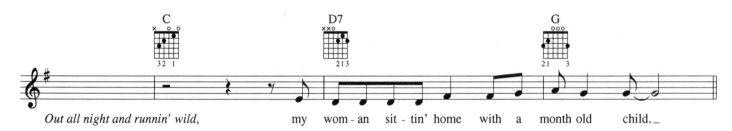

Out all night and runnin' wild, my wom-an sit-tin' home with a month old child._

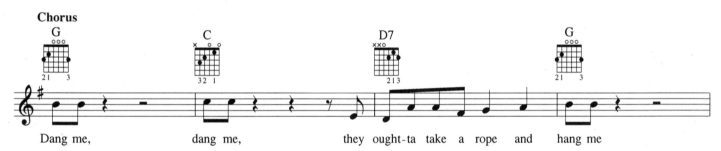

Dang me, dang me, they ought-ta take a rope and hang me

high from the high-est tree. Wom-an, would you weep for me? Do, do,__ do, do,_

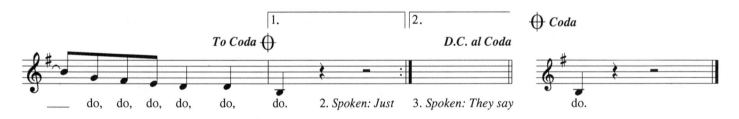

__ do, do, do, do, do, do. 2. *Spoken: Just* 3. *Spoken: They say* do.

Additional Lyrics

2. *Just sittin' round drinkin' with the rest of the guys,*
Six rounds bought and I bought five,
Spent the groceries and half the rent,
I lack fourteen dollars havin' twenty-seven cents.

3. *They say roses are red and violets are purple,*
Sugar's sweet and so is maple syruple,
Well, I'm the seventh out of seven sons,
My pappy was a pistol, I'm a son of a gun.

Detroit City

Words and Music by Danny Dill and Mel Tillis

Strum Pattern: 3
Pick Pattern: 3

Into
Moderately Fast

1. Last

Verse

night I went to sleep in De - troit cit - y   and I
2. See Additional Lyrics

dreamed a - bout the cot - ton fields and home. _____   I dreamed a - bout my

To Coda

moth - er,   dear old pa - pa,   sis - ter and broth - er   and I dreamed a - bout the girl who's been

Chorus

wait - ing for so long.   I wan - na go home, _____   I wan - na go

D.S. al Coda

home; _____   Oh, how I wan - na go home. _____

$\oplus$ *Coda*

read be-tween the lines. _____ I wan-na go home, _____ I wan-na go

home; _____ Oh, how I wan - na go home. _____

Additional Lyrics

2. Home folks think I'm big in Detroit city.
   From the letters that I write they think I'm fine.
   But by the day I make the cars, but night I make the bars;
   If only they could read between the lines.

Faded Love

Words and Music by Bob Wills and Johnny Wills

Strum Pattern: 3
Pick Pattern: 3

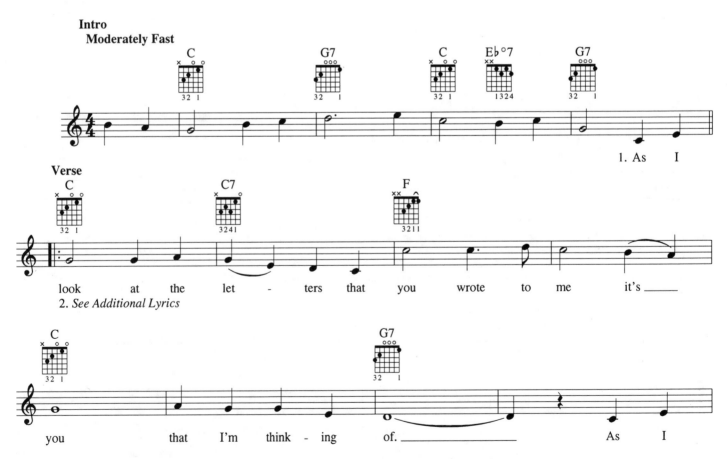

look at the let - ters that you wrote to me it's _____

2. See Additional Lyrics

you that I'm think - ing of. _____ As I

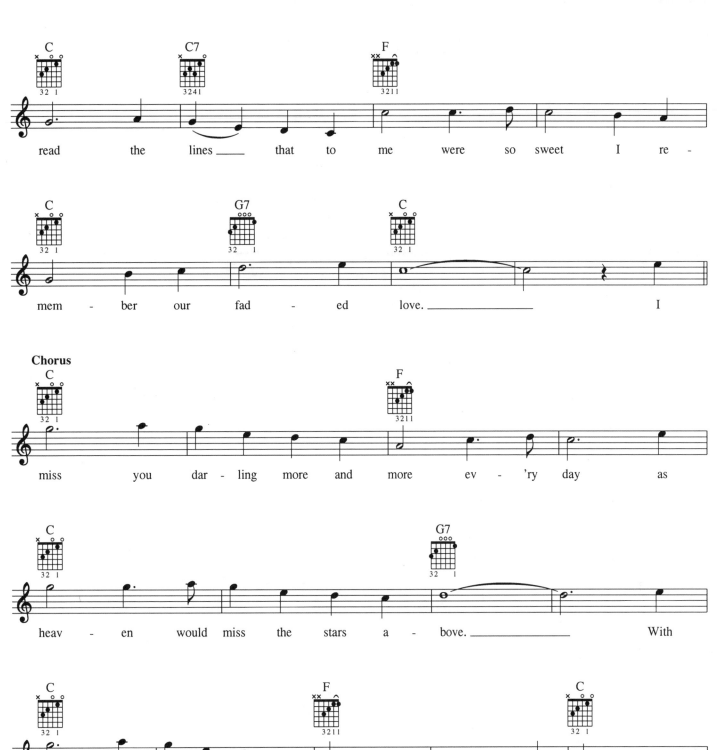

read   the   lines _____ that to me   were   so   sweet   I   re -

mem - ber   our   fad - ed   love. _____   I

Chorus

miss   you   dar - ling   more   and   more   ev - 'ry   day   as

heav - en   would miss   the   stars   a -   bove. _____   With

ev - 'ry   heart - beat I   still   think   of   you   and re - mem - ber   our

fad - ed love.   2. I _____ love. _____

Additional Lyrics

2. I think of the past and all the pleasures we had,
   As I watch the mating of the dove.
   It was in the springtime that you said goodbye,
   I remember our faded love.

D-I-V-O-R-C-E

Words and Music by Bobby Braddock and Curly Putman

Strum Pattern: 3
Pick Pattern: 3

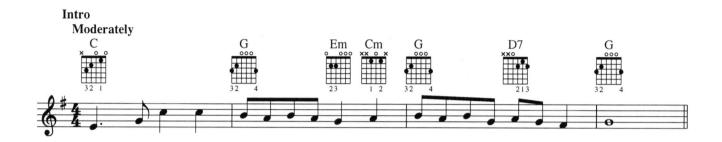

Intro
Moderately

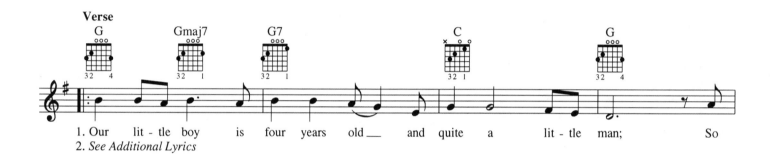

Verse

1. Our lit - tle boy is four years old ___ and quite a lit - tle man; So
2. *See Additional Lyrics*

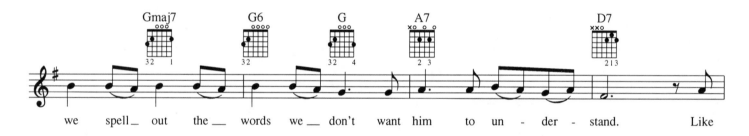

we spell ___ out the ___ words we ___ don't want him to un - der - stand. Like

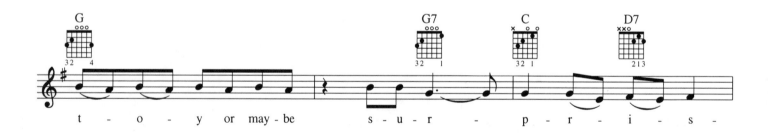

t - o - y or may - be s - u - r - p - r - i - s -

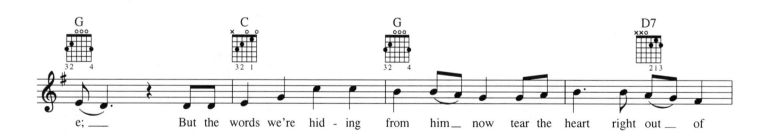

e; ___ But the words we're hid - ing from him ___ now tear the heart right out ___ of

me. Our d - i - v - o - r - c - e be - comes fi - nal to -

day; Me __ and __ lit - tle __ J - o - e will be go - ing a -

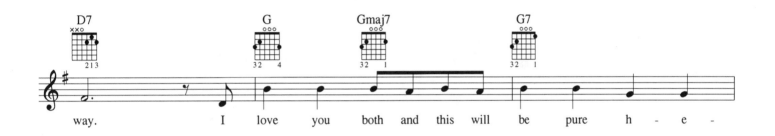

way. I love you both and this will be pure h - e -

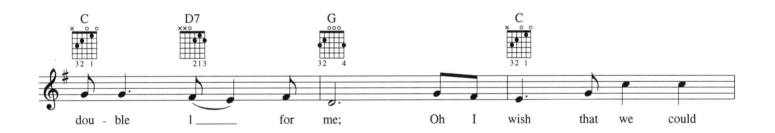

dou - ble l _____ for me; Oh I wish that we could

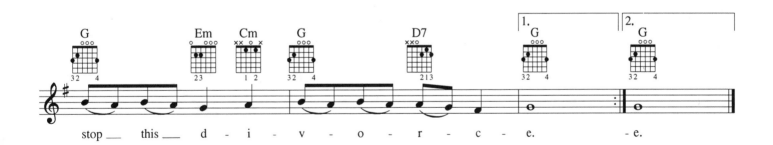

stop __ this __ d - i - v - o - r - c - e. - e.

Additional Lyrics

2. Watch him smile, he thinks it's Christmas or his fifth birthday;
And he thinks c - u - s - t - o - d - y spells fun or play.
I spell out all the hurtin' words and turn my head when I speak,
Because I can't spell away this hurt that's drippin' down my cheeks.

Easy Loving

Words and Music by Freddie Hart

Strum Pattern: 3
Pick Pattern: 3

Intro
Moderately

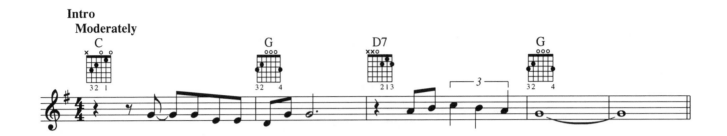

Verse

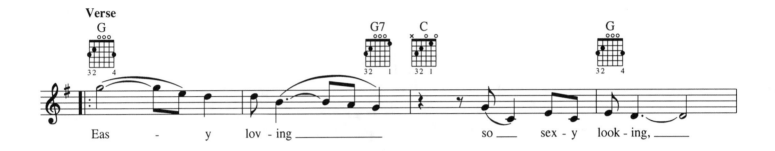

Eas - y lov - ing _____ so ___ sex - y look - ing, _____

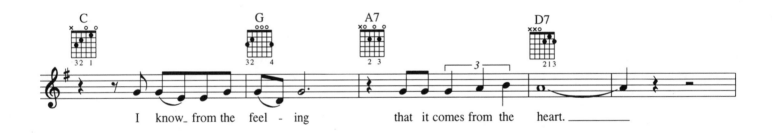

I know_ from the feel - ing that it comes from the heart. _____

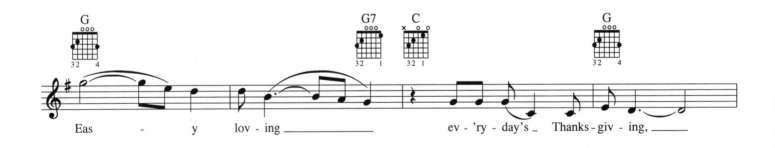

Eas - y lov - ing _____ ev - 'ry - day's _ Thanks - giv - ing, _____

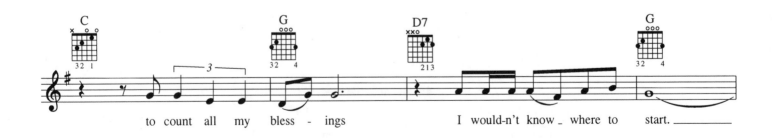

to count all my bless - ings I would-n't know _ where to start. _____

Ev - 'ry time _____ I look you o - ver, so real to life it

seems up - on your _ pret - ty shoul-ders there's a pair of an - gel

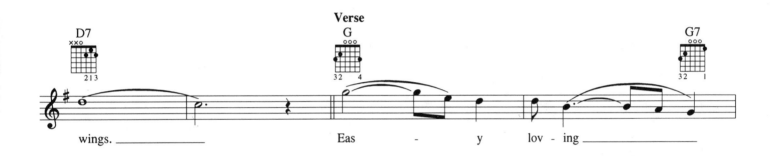

wings. _____ Eas - y lov - ing _____

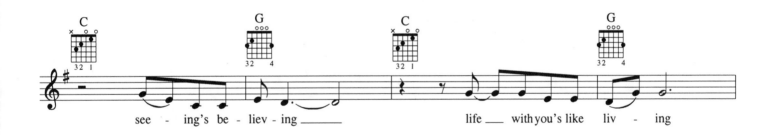

see - ing's be - liev - ing _____ life ___ with you's like liv - ing

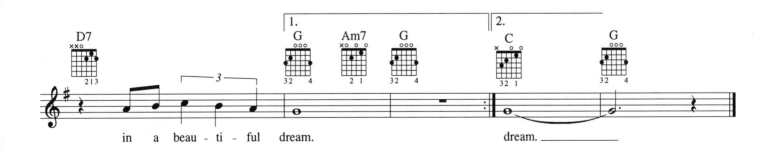

in a beau - ti - ful dream. dream. _____

El Paso

Words and Music by Marty Robbins

Strum Pattern: 8
Pick Pattern: 8

1. Out in the West Tex- as
2. *See Additional Lyrics*

town of El Pa- so, I fell in love with a Mex- i- can girl. _____

whirl. _____ 3. Black- er than night were the eyes of Fe- li- na, wick- ed and
6., 9., 12. *See Additional Lyrics*

e- vil while cast- ing a spell. _____ My love was deep for this Mex- i- can

maid- en, I was in love but in vain I could tell. _____

4. One night a wild young cow- boy came in wild as the West Tex- as
7., 10., 13. *See Additional Lyrics*

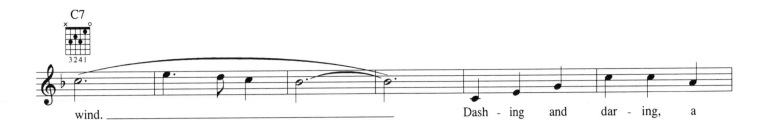

wind. _____ Dash - ing and dar - ing, a

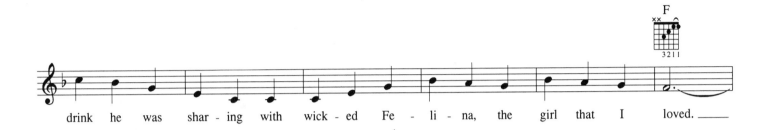

drink he was shar - ing with wick - ed Fe - li - na, the girl that I loved. _____

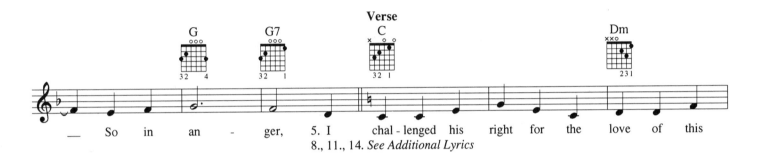

__ So in an - ger, 5. I chal - lenged his right for the love of this

8., 11., 14. *See Additional Lyrics*

maid - en, down went his hand for the gun that he wore. _____

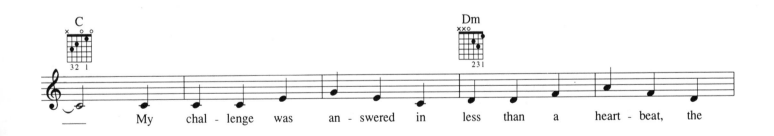

_____ My chal - lenge was an - swered in less than a heart - beat, the

play 4 times

hand - some young stran - ger lay dead on the floor. _____

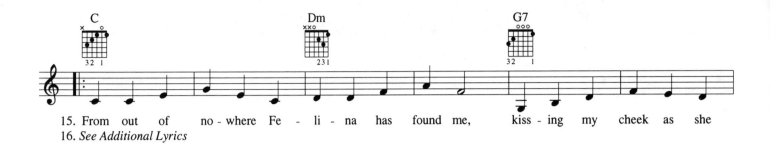

15. From out of no - where Fe - li - na has found me, kiss - ing my cheek as she
16. *See Additional Lyrics*

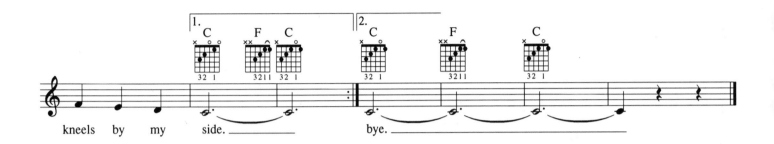

kneels by my side. _____ bye. _____

Additional Lyrics

2. Nightime would find me in Rosa's cantina,
   Music would play and Felina would whirl.

6. Just for a moment I stood there in silence,
   Shocked by the foul evil deed I had done.
   Many thoughts raced through my mind as I stood there,
   I had but one chance and that was to run.

7. Out through the back door of Rosa's I ran,
   Out where the horses were tied.
   I caught a good one it looked like it could run,
   Up on its back and away I did ride.

8. Just as fast as I could from the,
   West Texas town of El Paso,
   Out to the bad lands of New Mexico.
   (Instrumental)

9. Back in El Paso my life would be worthless,
   Ev'rything's gone, in life nothing's left.
   It's been so long since I've seen the young maiden,
   My love is stronger than my fear of death.

10. I saddled up and away I did go,
    Riding alone in the dark.
    Maybe tomorrow a bullet will find me,
    Tonight nothing's worse than this pain in my heart.
    And at last here I...

11. Am on the hill overlooking El Paso,
    I can see Rosa's cantina below.
    My love is strong and it pushes me onward,
    Down off the hill to Felina I go.

12. Off to my right I see five mounted cowboys,
    Off to my left ride a dozen or more.
    Shouting and shooting I can't let them catch me,
    I have to make it to Rosa's backdoor.

13. Something is dreadfully wrong,
    For I feel a deep burning pain in my side.
    Though I am trying to stay in the saddle,
    I'm getting weary, unable to ride.
    But my love for Fe...

14. Lina is strong, and I rise where I've fallen,
    Though I am weary I can't stop to rest.
    I see the white puff of smoke from the rifle,
    I feel the bullet go deep in my chest.

16. Cradled by two loving arms that I'll die for,
    One little kiss, then Felina goodbye.

Folsom Prison Blues

Words and Music by Johnny Cash

Strum Pattern: 3
Pick Pattern: 3

Additional Lyrics

2. When I was just a baby my mama told me son,
   Always be a good boy; don't ever play with guns.
   But I shot a man in Reno just to watch him die.
   When I hear that whistle blowin' I hang my head and cry.

3. I bet there's rich folks eatin' in a fancy dining car.
   They're prob'ly drinkin' coffee and smokin' big cigars.
   But I know I had it comin', I know I can't be free,
   But those people keep a-movin', and that's what tortures me.

4. Well, if they freed me from this prison, if that railroad train was mine,
   I bet I'd move on over a little farther down the line,
   Far from Folsom prison, that's where I want to stay.
   And I'd let that lonesome whistle blow my blues away.

The Fightin' Side of Me

Words and Music by Merle Haggard

Strum Pattern: 4
Pick Pattern: 5

Intro
Moderately Fast

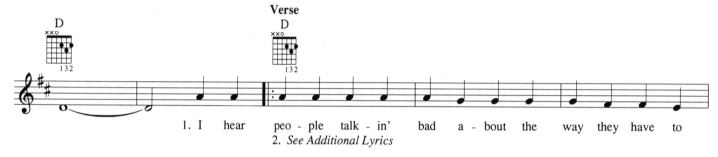

1. I hear peo - ple talk - in' bad a - bout the way they have to
2. *See Additional Lyrics*

live here in this coun - try. Harp - in' on the wars we fight

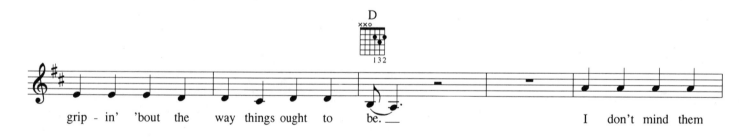

grip - in' 'bout the way things ought to be. ___ I don't mind them

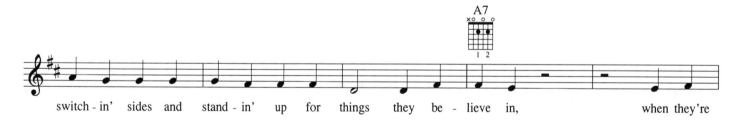

switch - in' sides and stand - in' up for things they be - lieve in, when they're

run - nin' down our coun - try man they're walk - in' on the fight - in' side of me.

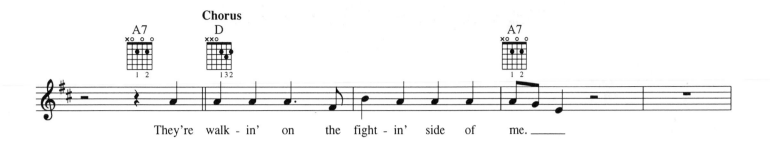

They're walk - in' on the fight - in' side of me. _____

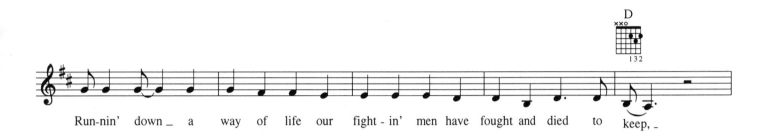

Run - nin' down _ a way of life our fight - in' men have fought and died to keep, _

if you don't love it, leave it, let this song _ that I'm sing - in' be a

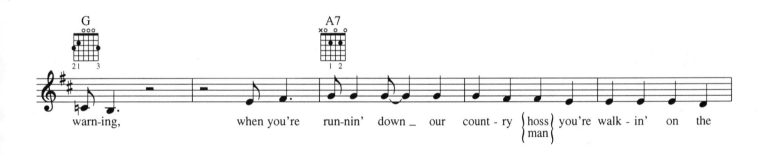

warn - ing, when you're run - nin' down _ our coun - try { hoss / man } you're walk - in' on the

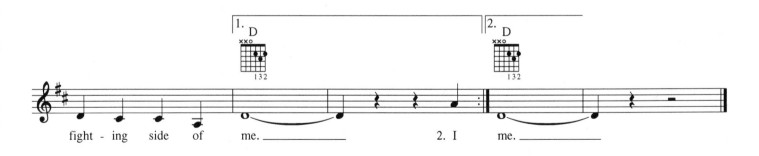

1.
fight - ing side of me. _____ 2. I

2.
me. _____

Additional lyrics

2. I read about some squirley guy who claims he just don't believe in fightin',
   And I wonder just how long the rest of us can count on bein' free.
   They love our milk and honey but they preach about some other way of livin',
   When they're runnin' down our country man they're walkin' on the fightin' side of me.

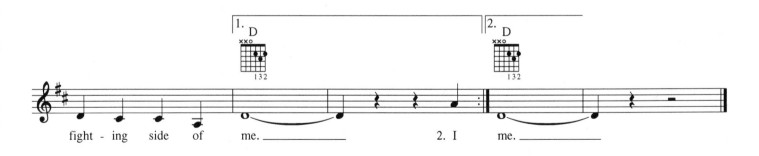

Flowers on the Wall

Words and Music by Lewis DeWitt

Strum Pattern: 6
Pick Pattern: 6

1. I've been hear - in' you're con - cerned a - bout my hap - pi - ness, ___ but
2. *See Additional Lyrics*

all that thought ___ you're giv - in' me ___ is con - science I guess. ___ If

I were walk - in' in your shoes, _ I would-n't wor - ry none. ___ While

you and your friends ___ are wor - ryin' 'bout me ___ I'm hav - in' lots of fun ___

___ count - in' flow - ers on the wall, ___ that don't both - er me at all, ___

play - in' sol - i - tare ___ till dawn ___ with a

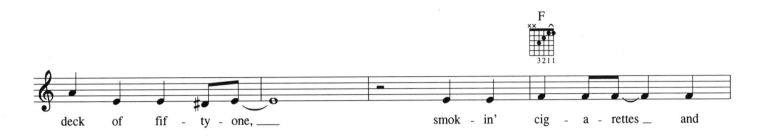

deck of fif - ty - one, ___ smok - in' cig - a - rettes ___ and

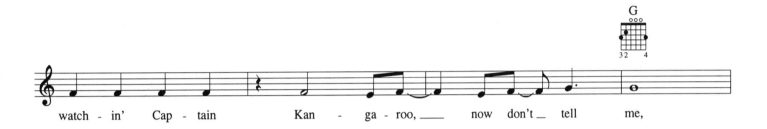

watch - in' Cap - tain Kan - ga - roo, ___ now don't ___ tell me,

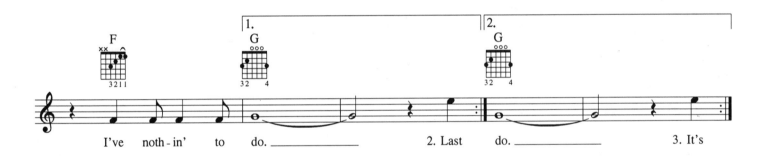

I've noth - in' to do. ___ 2. Last do. ___ 3. It's

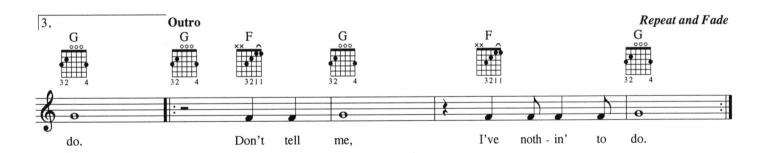

do. Don't tell me, I've noth - in' to do.

Additional Lyrics

2. Last night I dressed in tails, pretended I was on the town;
As long as I can dream it's hard to slow this swinger down.
So please don't give a thought to me, I'm really doin' fine,
You can always find me here and having quite a time...

3. It's good to see you, I must go, I know I look a fright;
Anyway my eyes are not accustomed to this light.
And my shoes are not accustomed to this hard time street,
So I must go back to my room and make my day complete...

(Now and Then There's)
A Fool Such as I

Words and Music by Bil Trader

Strum Pattern: 3
Pick Pattern: 3

MCA music publishing

I am _____ o - ver you. You taught me how _ to love, and now _

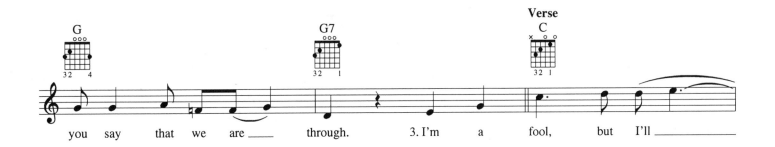

you say that we are _____ through. 3. I'm a fool, but I'll _____

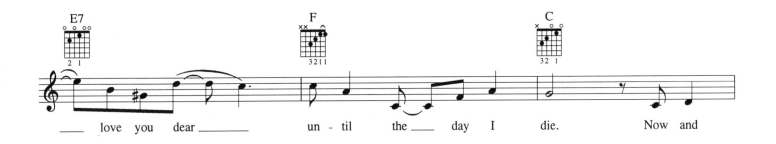

_____ love you dear _____ un - til the _ day I die. Now and

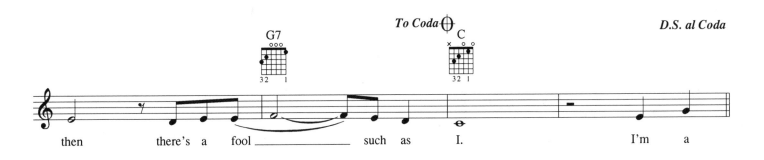

To Coda ✛   *D.S. al Coda*

then there's a fool _____ such as I. I'm a

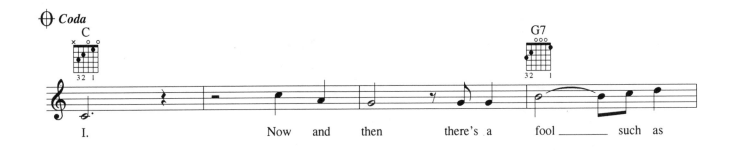

✛ *Coda*

I. Now and then there's a fool _____ such as

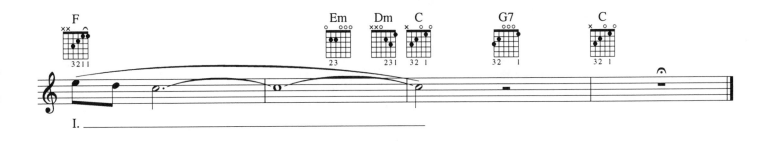

I. _____

Funny How Time Slips Away

Words and Music by Willie Nelson

Strum Pattern: 3
Pick Pattern: 4

1. Well, hel - lo there, my it's been a long, long
2., 3. *See Additional Lyrics*

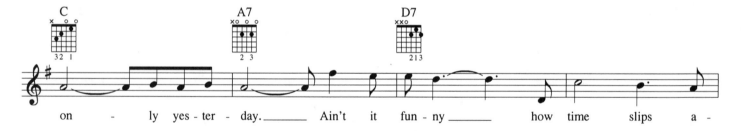

time. _____ "How'm I do - in'?" _____ Oh, I guess that I'm do - in'

fine. _____ It's been so long now _____ yet it seems like it was

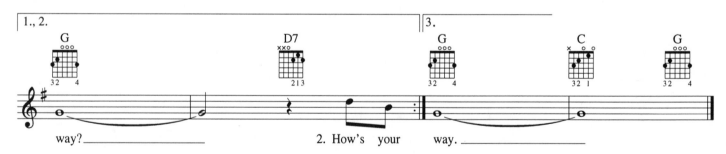

on - ly yes - ter - day. _____ Ain't it fun - ny _____ how time slips a -

1., 2. way? _____ **3.** 2. How's your way. _____

Additional Lyrics

2. How's your new love, I hope that he's doin' fine.
   Heard you told him that you'd love him 'til the end of time.
   Now, that's the same thing that you told me, seems like only yesterday.
   Ain't it funny how time slips away?

3. Gotta go now, guess I'll see you around.
   Don't know when though, never know when I'll be back in town.
   Just remember what I tell you, that in time you're gonna pay.
   And it's surprising how time slips away.

Funny Way of Laughin'

Words and Music by Hank Cochran

Strum Pattern: 2
Pick Pattern: 5

Additional Lyrics

2. If we meet on the street and a little bitty tear rolls down my cheek,
   Please don't think it's because I'm blue, or that I'm still in love with you.

3. Remember the day you left our place and how the tears rolled down my face?
   It wasn't because you were leavin' me, I was happy because you were pleasing me.

The Gambler

Words and Music by Don Schlitz

Strum Pattern: 4
Pick Pattern: 5

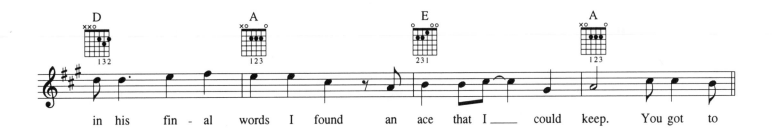

in his fin - al words I found an ace that I ____ could keep. You got to

Chorus

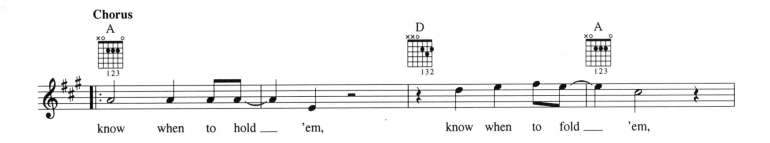

know when to hold ____ 'em, know when to fold ____ 'em,

know when to walk ____ a - way ____ and know when to run. ____ You nev - er

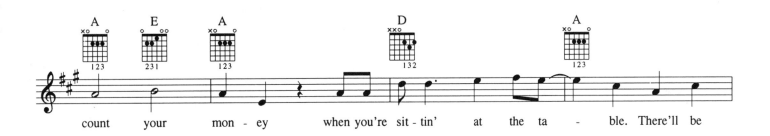

count your mon - ey when you're sit - tin' at the ta - ble. There'll be

time e - nough ____ for count - in' when the deal - in's done. You got to done.

Additional Lyrics

2. He said, "Son I've made a life out of readin' peoples faces,
And knowing what their cards were by the way they held their eyes.
And if you don't mind my sayin' I can see you're out of aces,
For a taste of whiskey I'll give you some advice."

Gentle on My Mind

Words and Music by John Hartford

Strum Pattern: 3
Pick Pattern: 3

𝄋 **Verse**
Moderately Fast

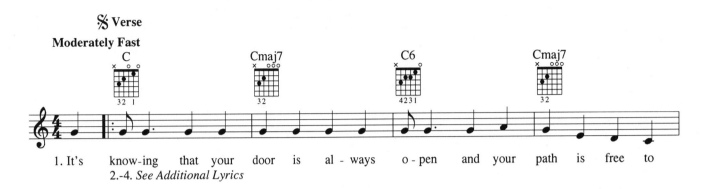

1. It's know-ing that your door is al-ways o-pen and your path is free to
2.-4. *See Additional Lyrics*

walk, that makes me tend to

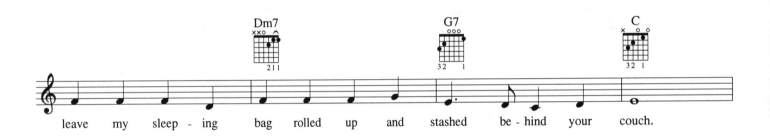

leave my sleep-ing bag rolled up and stashed be-hind your couch.

And it's know-ing I'm not shack-led by for-

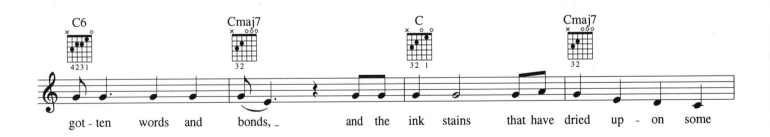

got-ten words and bonds, __ and the ink stains that have dried up-on some

line,   that   keeps   you   in   the

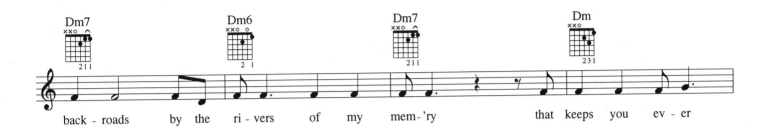

back - roads   by   the   ri - vers   of   my   mem-'ry   that   keeps   you   ev - er

gen - tle   on   my   mind.   2. It's   mind. _____

Additional Lyrics

2. It's not clinging to the rocks and ivy planted on their columns now that binds me,
   Or something that somebody said because they thought we fit together walkin'.
   It's just knowing that the world will not be cursing or forgiving when I walk along
   Some railroad track and find,
   That you're moving on the backroads by the rivers of my memory and for hours,
   You're just gentle on my mind.

3. Though the wheat fields and the clothes lines and junkyards and the highways
   Come between us,
   And some other woman crying to her mother 'cause she turned and I was gone.
   I still run in silence, tears of joy might stain my face and summer sun might
   Burn me 'til I'm blind,
   But not to where I cannot see you walkin' on the backroads by the rivers flowing
   Gentle on my mind.

4. I dip my cup of soup back from the gurglin' cauldron in some train yard.
   My beard a roughning coal pile and a dirty hat pulled low across my face.
   Though cupped hands 'round a tin can I pretend I hold you to my breast and find,
   That you're waving from the backroads by the rivers of my memory ever smilin',
   Ever gentle on my mind.

Golden Ring

Words and Music by Bobby Braddock and Rafe VanHoy

Strum Pattern: 2
Pick Pattern: 3

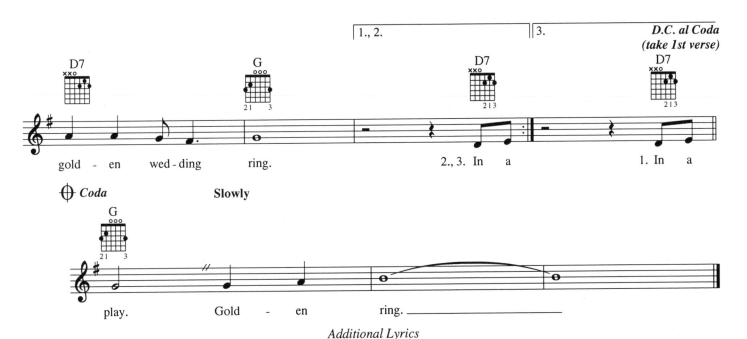

gold - en wed-ding ring.

2., 3. In a

1. In a

Coda   **Slowly**

play.   Gold - en   ring.

Additional Lyrics

2. In a little wedding chapel later on that afternoon,
   An old upright piano plays that old familiar tune.
   Tears roll down her cheeks and happy thoughts run through her head,
   As he whispers low, "With this ring I thee wed."

Chorus Golden ring, with one tiny little stone,
          Shining ring, now at last it's found a home.
          By itself, it's just a cold metallic thing.
          Only love can make a golden wedding ring.

3. In a small two room apartment, as they fight their final round,
   He says, "You won't admit it, but I know you're leavin' town."
   She says, "One thing's for certain, I don't love you anymore,"
   And throws down the ring as she walks out the door.

Chorus Golden ring, with one tiny little stone,
          Cast aside, like the love that's dead and gone.
          By itself, it's just a cold metallic thing.
          Only love can make a golden wedding ring.

The Happiest Girl in the Whole U.S.A.

Words and Music by Donna Fargo

Strum Pattern: 8
Pick Pattern: 8

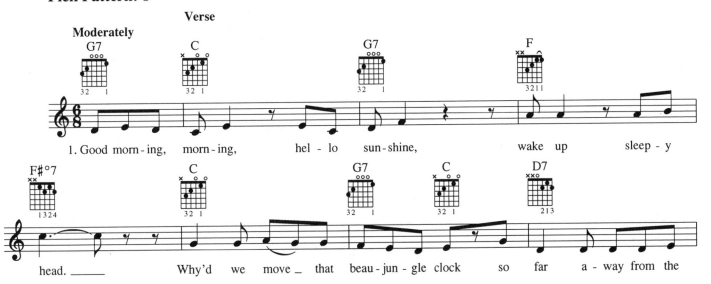

1. Good morn-ing, morn-ing, hel-lo sun-shine, wake up sleep-y

head. _____ Why'd we move _ that beau-jun-gle clock so far a-way from the

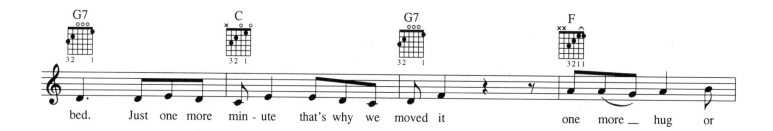

bed. Just one more min - ute that's why we moved it one more ___ hug or

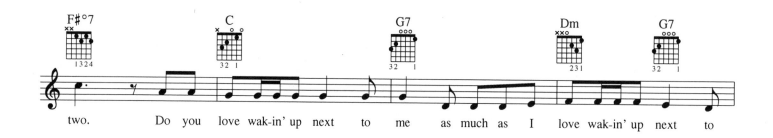

two. Do you love wak-in' up next to me as much as I love wak-in' up next to

Verse

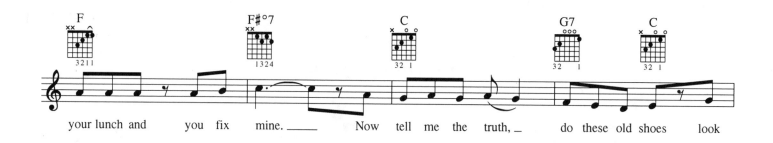

you. _____ 2. You make the cof - fee I'll make the bed, I'll fix

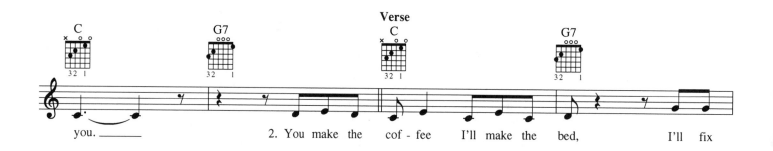

your lunch and you fix mine. _____ Now tell me the truth, _ do these old shoes look

Pre-Chorus

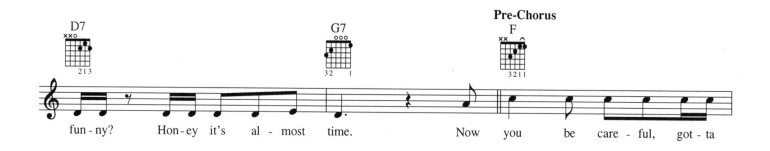

fun - ny? Hon - ey it's al - most time. Now you be care - ful, got - ta

Chorus

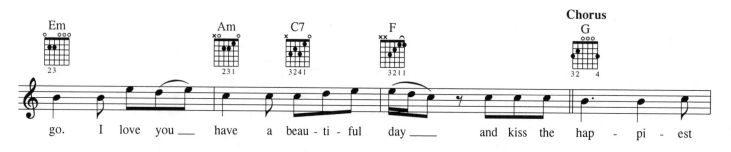

go. I love you ___ have a beau - ti - ful day ___ and kiss the hap - pi - est

girl _____ in the whole _____ U. S. A.   Skip - a - dee - doo - dah, ___

thank you, Lord, for mak - ing him for me. _____ And thank you for let - ting life

turn out the way   that I al - ways thought it could be. _____ There

once was a time when I could not i - mag - ine ___ how it would feel ___ to say   I'm the

hap - pi - est girl ___   in the whole _____ U. S. A. _____   Now;

Outro

Shine on me sun - shine walk with me world, it's a skip - a - dee - doo - dah, day,   and I'm the

Repeat and Fade

hap - pi - est girl ___   in the whole ____ U. S. A. ____

Have I Told You Lately That I Love You

Words and Music by Scott Wiseman

Strum Pattern: 2
Pick Pattern: 4

Verse
Moderately Fast

1. Have I told you late-ly that I love you? _____ Could I
2., 3. *See Additional Lyrics*

tell you once a-gain some-how? _____ Have I told with all my heart and

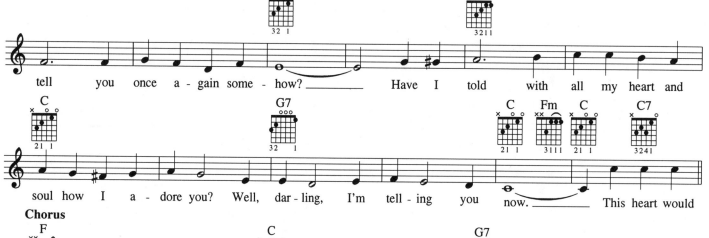

soul how I a-dore you? Well, dar-ling, I'm tell-ing you now. _____ This heart would

Chorus

break in two if you re-fuse me. _____ I'm no good with-out you an-y-

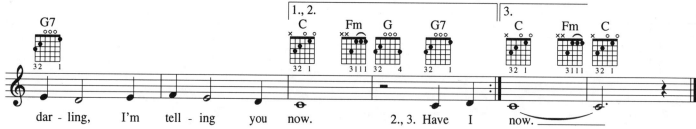

how. _____ Dear, have I told you late-ly that I love you? _____ Well,

dar-ling, I'm tell-ing you now. 2., 3. Have I now. _____

Additional Lyrics

2. Have I told you lately how I miss you
   When the stars are shining in the sky?
   Have I told you why the nights are long when you're not with me?
   Well, darling, I'm telling you now.

3. Have I told you lately when I'm sleeping
   Ev'ry dream I dream is you somehow?
   Have I told you I'd like to share my love forever?
   Well, darling, I'm telling you now.

MCA music publishing

He Stopped Loving Her Today

Words and Music by Bobby Braddock and Curly Putman

Strum Pattern: 1
Pick Pattern: 4

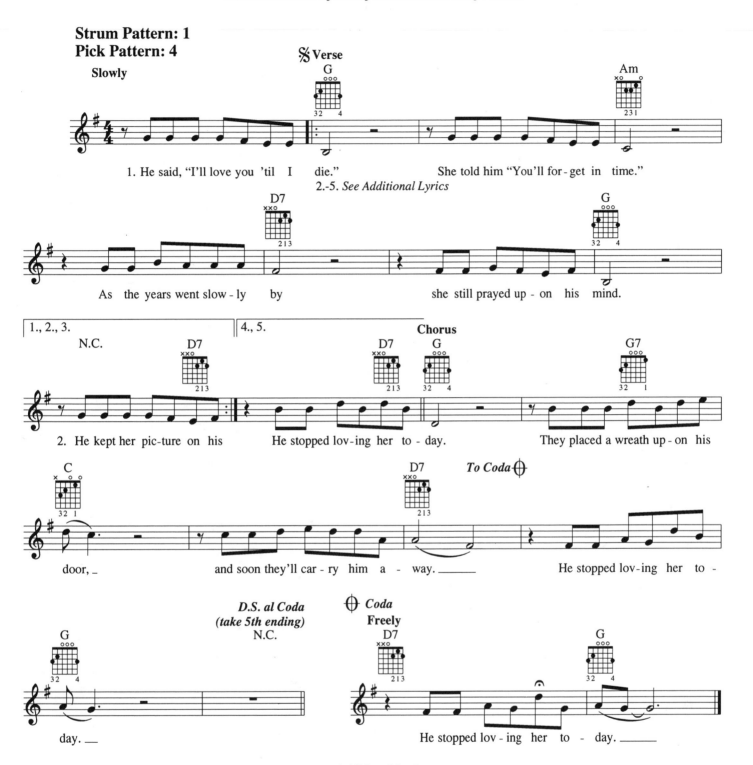

Additional Lyrics

2. He kept her picture on his wall; went half crazy now and then,
   But he still loved her through it all, hoping she'd come back again.

3. He kept some letters by his bed, dated 1962.
   He had underlined in red ev'ry single "I love you."

4. I went to see him just today, oh, but I didn't see no tears.
   All dressed up to go away, first time I'd seen him smile in years.

5. *Spoken: You know, she came to see him one last time.*
   We all wondered if she would.
   And it kept running through my mind,
   This time he's over her for good.

Heartaches by the Number

Words and Music by Harlan Howard

Strum Pattern: 2
Pick Pattern: 1

Additional Lyrics

2. Heartache number three was when you called me,
   And said that you were coming back to stay.
   With hopeful heart I waited for your knock on the door.
   I waited but you must have lost your way.

Hello Walls

Words and Music by Willie Nelson

Strum Pattern: 1
Pick Pattern: 4

Additional Lyrics

2. Hello, window, well, I see that you're still here.
   Aren't you lonely since our darlin' disappeared?
   Well, look here, is that a teardrop in the corner of your pane?
   Now, don't you try to tell me that it's rain.

3. Hello, ceiling. I'm gonna stare at you a while.
   You know I can't sleep, so won't you bear with me a while?
   We must all pull together or else I'll lose my mind.
   'Cause I've got a feelin' she'll be gone a long, long time.

Help Me Make It Through the Night

Words and Music by Kris Kristofferson

Strum Pattern: 2
Pick Pattern: 4

Additional Lyrics

2. Come and lay down by my side,
   'Til the mornin' light.
   All I'm takin' is your time.

3. Yesterday is dead and gone,
   And tomorrow's out of sight,
   And it's sad to be alone.

Hey, Good Lookin'

Words and Music by Hank Williams

Strum Pattern: 3
Pick Pattern: 3

To Coda ⊕

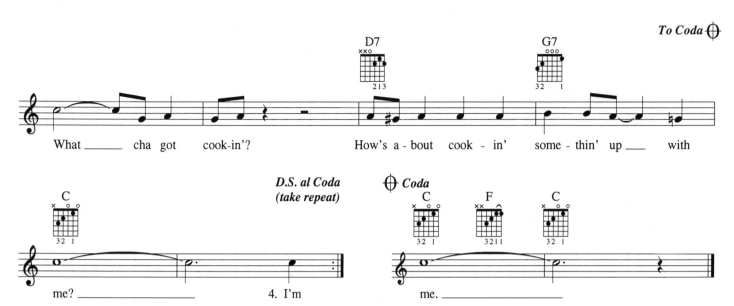

What ___ cha got cook-in'? How's a-bout cook-in' some-thin' up ___ with

D.S. al Coda
(take repeat)

⊕ **Coda**

me? _____ 4. I'm

me. _____

Additional Lyrics

Chorus 2. Hey, sweet baby, don't you think maybe,
We could find us a brand new recipe?

4. I'm free and ready so we can go steady.
How's about saving all your time for me?

5. No more lookin', know I've been tooken.
How's about keepin' steady company?

Verse 2. I'm gonna throw my date book over the fence,
And find me one for five or ten cents.
I'll keep it 'til it's covered with age,
Cause I'm writin' your name down on ev'ry page.

Honky Tonk Blues

Words and Music by Hank Williams

Strum Pattern: 3
Pick Pattern: 3

Verse
Moderately

1. I left my home ___ down on a ru-ral route ___ and told my folks ___ I'm go-in'
3., 5. *See Additional Lyrics*

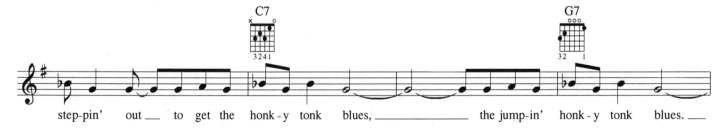

step-pin' out ___ to get the honk-y tonk blues, _____ the jump-in' honk-y tonk blues. ___

Lord, I got 'em _____ I got the honk - y tonk blues.

Verse

2. I went to _____ a dance, wore out my shoes, _ woke up this morn - in' wish - in'
4., 6. *See Additional Lyrics*

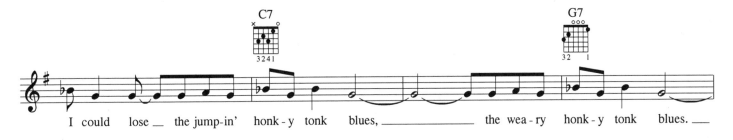

I could lose _ the jump-in' honk - y tonk blues, _____ the wea - ry honk - y tonk blues. _

_____ Lord I'm suf - ferin' _____ with the honk - y tonk blues.

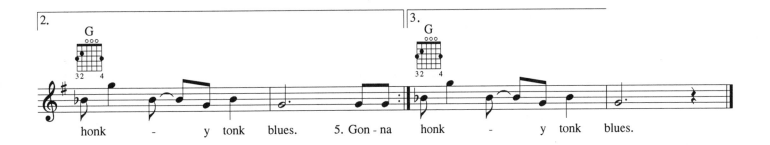

honk - y tonk blues. 5. Gon - na honk - y tonk blues.

Additional Lyrics

3. I stopped into ev'ry place in town, this city life has really got me down.
I got the honky tonk blues, I got the honky tonk blues.
Lord I'm sufferin' with the honky tonk blues.

4. When I get home again to ma and pa, I know they're gonna lay down,
Down the law about the honky tonk blues, the jumpin' honky tonk blues.
Lord I'm sufferin' with the honky tonk blues.

5. Gonna tuck my worries underneath my arm, and get right back to my pappy's farm,
And leave the honky tonk blues, forget the honky tonk blues.
I don't want to be bothered with the honky tonk blues.

6. When I get home again to ma and pa, I know they're gonna lay down,
Down the law about the honky tonk blues, the jumpin' honky tonk blues.
Lord I'm sufferin' with the honky tonk blues.

I Fall to Pieces

Words and Music by Hank Cochran and Harlan Howard

Strum Pattern: 3
Pick Pattern: 3

Additional Lyrics

Chorus 2. I fall to pieces each time someone speaks your name.
I fall to pieces. Time only adds to the flame.

Verse 2. You tell me to find someone else to love,
Someone who'll love me too, the way you used to do.
But each time I go out with someone new,
You walk by and I fall to pieces.

I Walk the Line

Words and Music by Johnny Cash

Strum Pattern: 4
Pick Pattern: 5

Intro
Moderately Fast

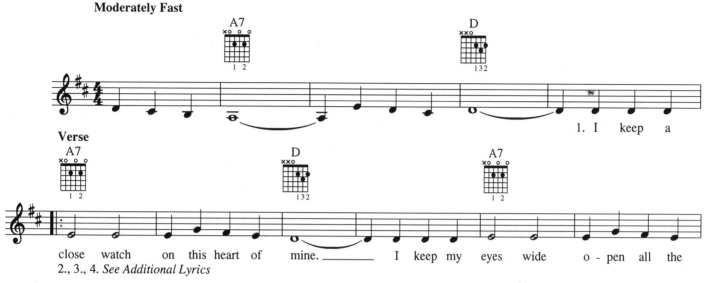

Verse

close watch on this heart of mine. _____ I keep my eyes wide o - pen all the
2., 3., 4. *See Additional Lyrics*

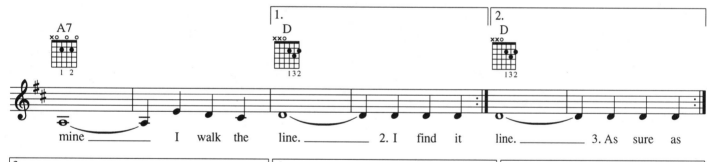

time. _____ I keep the ends out for the time that binds. _____ Be - cause you're

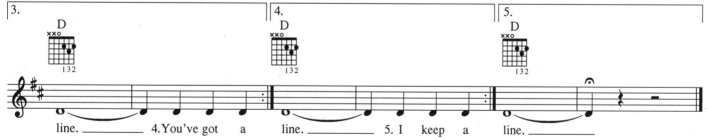

mine _____ I walk the line. _____ 2. I find it line. _____ 3. As sure as

line. _____ 4.You've got a line. _____ 5. I keep a line. _____

Additional Lyrics

2. I find it very easy to be true.
   I find myself alone when each day is through.
   Yes, I'll admit that I'm a fool for you.
   Because you're mine I walk the line.

3. As sure as night is dark and day is light,
   I keep you on my mind both day and night.
   And happiness I've known proves that it's right.

4. You've got a way to keep me on your side.
   You give me cause for love that I can't hide.
   For you I know I'd even try to turn the tide.
   Because you're mine I walk the line.

5. I keep a close watch on this heart of mine.
   I keep my eyes wide open all the time.
   I keep the ends out for the tie that binds.
   Because you're mine I walk the line.

I'm Not Lisa

Words and Music by Jessi Colter

Strum Pattern: 3
Pick Pattern: 3

1. I'm not Li - sa; my name is Ju - lie.
2. *See Additional Lyrics*

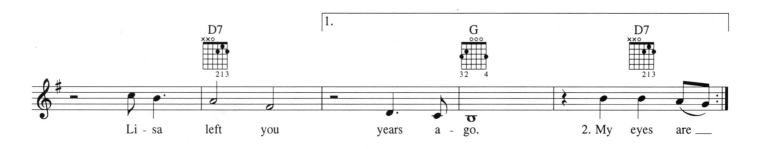

Li - sa left you years a - go. 2. My eyes are ___

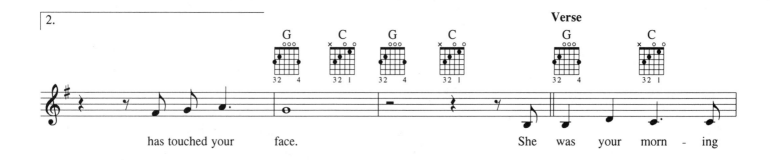

has touched your face. She was your morn - ing

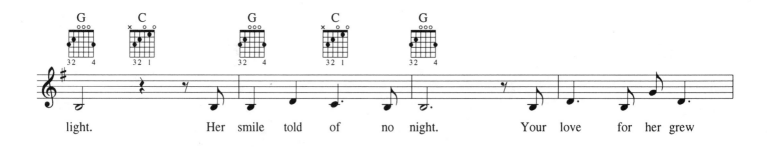

light. Her smile told of no night. Your love for her grew

with each ris - ing sun, _____ and then one win - ter

Additional Lyrics

Chorus 2. My eyes are not blue, but mine won't leave you,
'Til the sunlight has touched your face.

Chorus 4. My eyes are not blue, but mine won't leave you,
'Til the sunlight shines through your face.

If We Make It Through December

Words and Music by Merle Haggard

Strum Pattern: 4
Pick Pattern: 5

Additional Lyrics

2. If we make it through December,
   Got plans to be a warmer town come summertime;
   Maybe even California.
   If we make it through December, we'll be fine.

I'm So Lonesome I Could Cry

Words and Music by Hank Williams

Strum Pattern: 8
Pick Pattern: 8

Additional Lyrics

2. I've never seen a night so long, when time goes crawling by,
   The moon just went behind a cloud, to hide its face and cry.

3. Did you ever see a robin weep when leaves began to die?
   That means he's lost the will to live.
   I'm so lonely I could cry.

4. The silence of a falling star lights up a purple sky.
   And as I wonder where you are,
   I'm so lonely I could cry.

Islands in the Stream

Words and Music by Barry Gibb, Maurice Gibb and Robin Gibb

Strum Pattern: 3
Pick Pattern: 3

ride it to-ge-ther ah ah,_____ ma-kin' love _____ with each oth-er ah

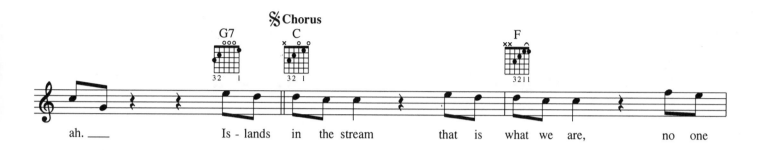

§ Chorus

ah. _____ Is - lands in the stream that is what we are, no one

in be - tween. How can we be wrong? Sail a - way with me to an -

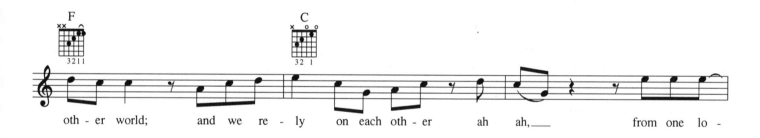

oth - er world; and we re - ly on each oth - er ah ah,_____ from one lo -

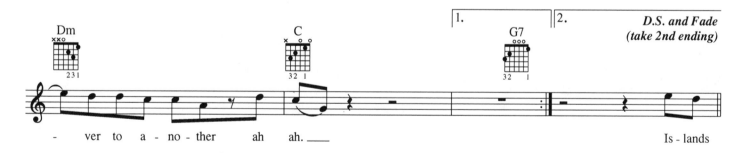

1.　　　　2.　　　　*D.S. and Fade*
(take 2nd ending)

- ver to a - no - ther ah ah. _____　　　　Is - lands

Additional Lyrics

2. I can't live without you if the love was gone.
   Ev'rything is nothing if you got no one,
   And you did walk in the night, slowly losing sight of the real thing.
   But, that won't happen to us and we got no doubt,
   Too deep in love and we got no way out and the message is clear,
   This could be the year for the real thing.
   No more will you cry. Baby I will hurt you never.
   We start and end as one in love forever.
   We can ride it together ah ah,
   Makin' love with each other ah ah.

It Was Almost Like a Song

Lyrics by Hal David, Music by Archie Jordan

Strum Pattern: 5
Pick Pattern: 4

year;   Then the flame be - came a dy - ing ____ em - ber;

Chorus

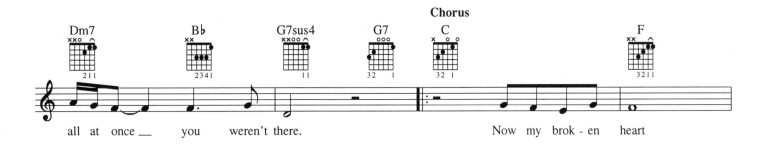

all at once ____ you weren't there.   Now my brok - en heart

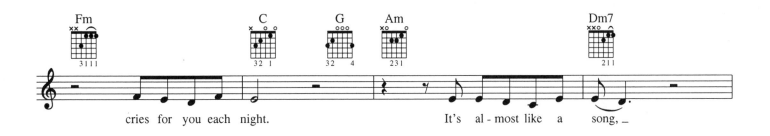

cries for you each night.   It's al - most like a song, __

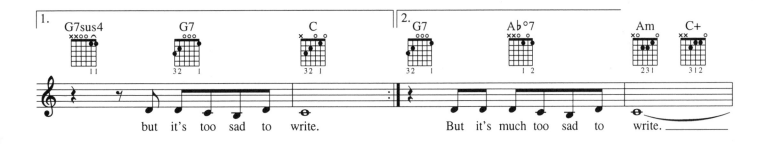

1. but it's too sad to write.   **2.** But it's much too sad to write. ____

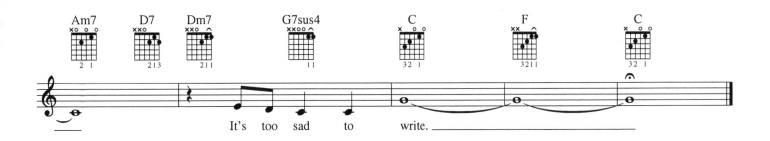

____ It's too sad to write. ____

Additional Lyrics

2. You were in my arms,
    Just where you belong.
    We were so in love.
    It was almost like a song.

Jambalaya (On the Bayou)

Words and Music by Hank Williams

Strum Pattern: 3
Pick Pattern: 3

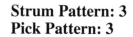

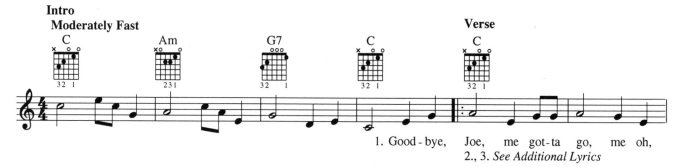

1. Good-bye, Joe, me got-ta go, me oh,
2., 3. *See Additional Lyrics*

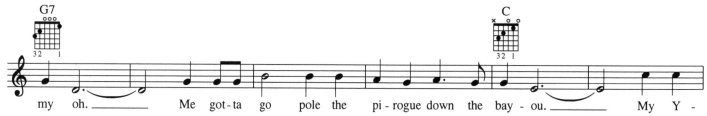

my oh. ____ Me got-ta go pole the pi-rogue down the bay-ou. ____ My Y-

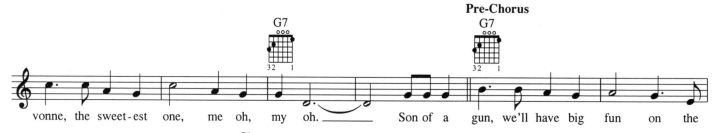

vonne, the sweet-est one, me oh, my oh. ____ Son of a gun, we'll have big fun on the

bay-ou. ____ Jam-ba-la-ya and a craw-fish pie and fil-let gum-bo, ____ 'cause to-

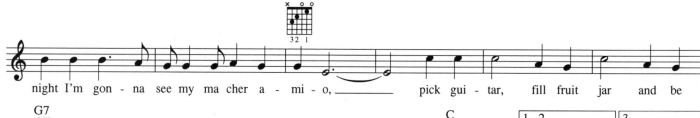

night I'm gon-na see my ma cher a-mi-o, ____ pick gui-tar, fill fruit jar and be

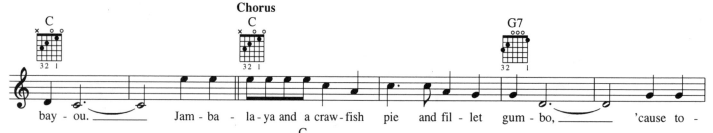

gay-o. ____ Son of a gun, we'll have big fun on the bay-ou. ____ 2. Thi-bo

Additional Lyrics

2. Thi bo daux, Fontaineaux, the place is buzzin'.
   Kinfolk come to see Yvonne by the dozen.
   Dress in style and go hog wild, me oh, my oh.

3. Settle down far from town, get me a pirogue,
   And I'll catch all the fish in the bayou.
   Swap my mon to buy Yvonne what we need-o.

It's Not Love
(But It's Not Bad)

Words and Music by Glenn Martin and Hank Cochran

Strum Pattern: 2
Pick Pattern: 2

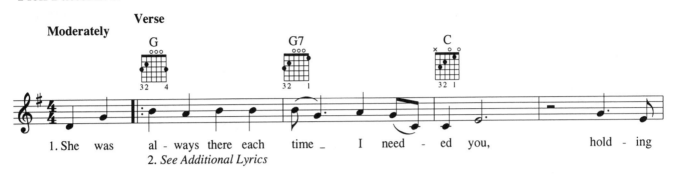

1. She was al - ways there each time I need - ed you, hold - ing
2. *See Additional Lyrics*

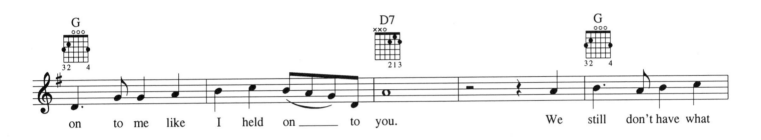

on to me like I held on to you. We still don't have what

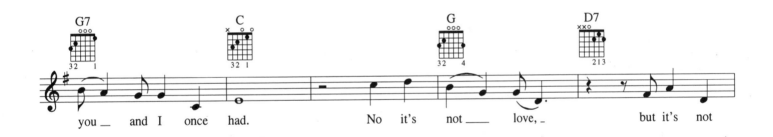

you and I once had. No it's not love, but it's not

bad. No it's not love, not like ours was.

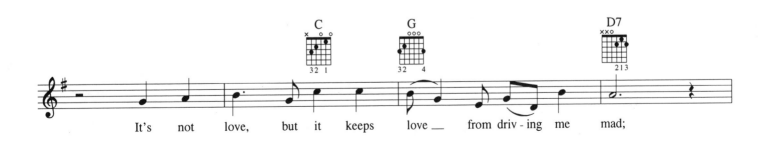

It's not love, but it keeps love from driv-ing me mad;

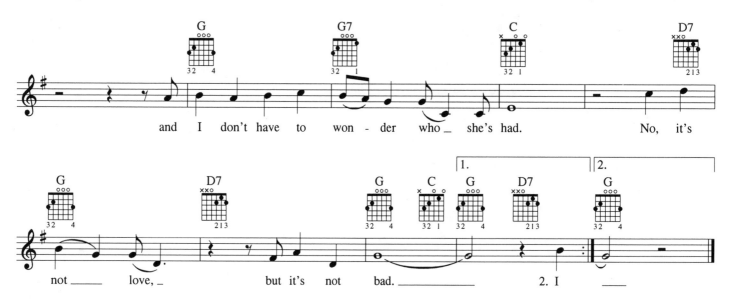

and I don't have to won - der who _ she's had.   No, it's
not _____ love, _   but it's not bad. _____   1.   2. I _____
2. I

Additional Lyrics

2. I turn to her when you leave me alone,
   Sometimes even when you're here, and you're still gone.
   She's slowly changing what you leave so sad.
   No, it's not love, but it's not bad.

The Last Word in Lonesome Is Me

Words and Music by Roger Miller

Strum Pattern: 8
Pick Pattern: 8

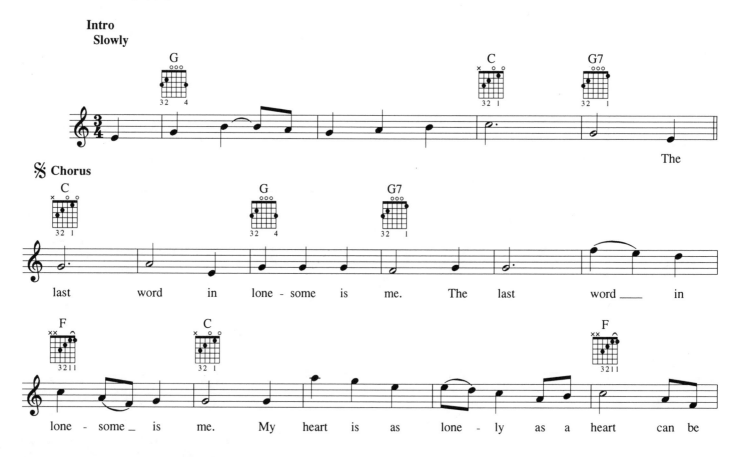

Intro
Slowly

The

% Chorus

last   word   in   lone - some   is   me.   The   last   word _____   in

lone - some _ is   me.   My   heart   is   as   lone - ly   as   a   heart   can   be

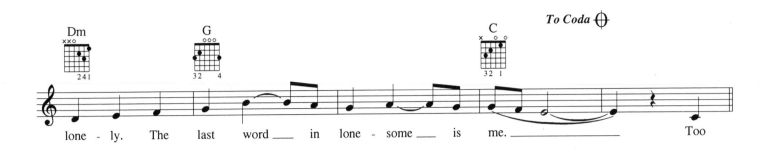

To Coda ⊕

lone - ly. The last word __ in lone - some __ is me. _____ Too

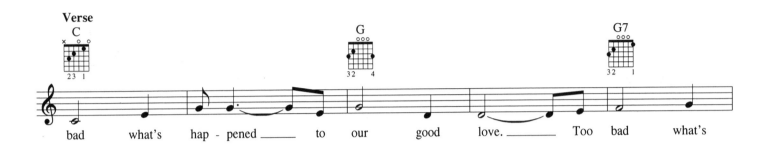

Verse

bad what's hap - pened _____ to our good love. _____ Too bad what's

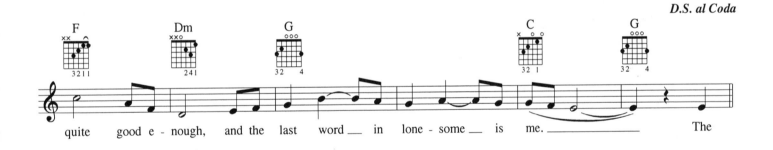

hap - pened _____ to our good love. Some - times our best is - n't

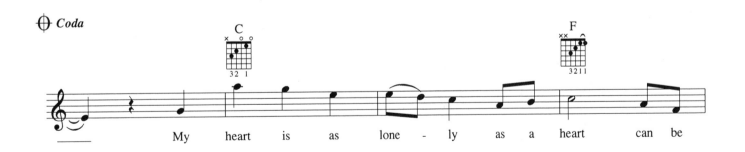

D.S. al Coda

quite good e - nough, and the last word __ in lone - some __ is me. _____ The

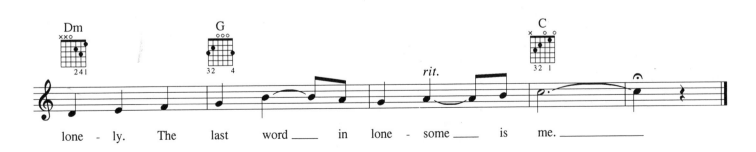

⊕ *Coda*

_____ My heart is as lone - ly as a heart can be

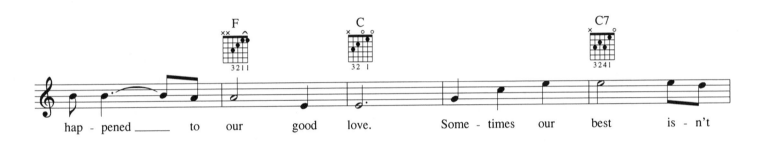

lone - ly. The last word __ in lone - some __ is me. _____

rit.

King of the Road

Words and Music by Roger Miller

Strum Pattern: 4
Pick Pattern: 5

Verse
Moderately

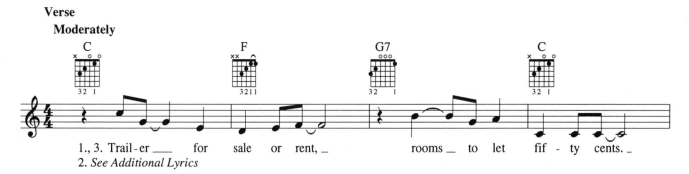

1., 3. Trail-er ___ for sale or rent, _ rooms _ to let fif - ty cents. _
2. *See Additional Lyrics*

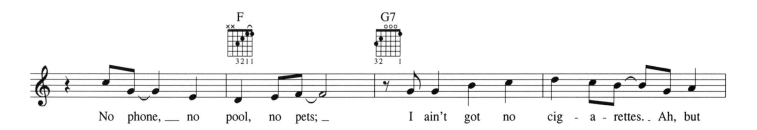

No phone, _ no pool, no pets; _ I ain't got no cig - a - rettes. _ Ah, but

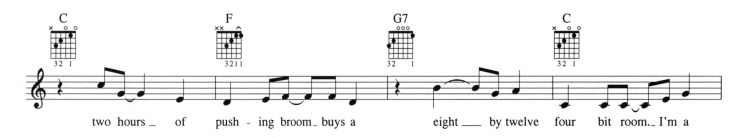

two hours _ of push - ing broom _ buys a eight ___ by twelve four bit room. _ I'm a

To Coda ⊕   1.

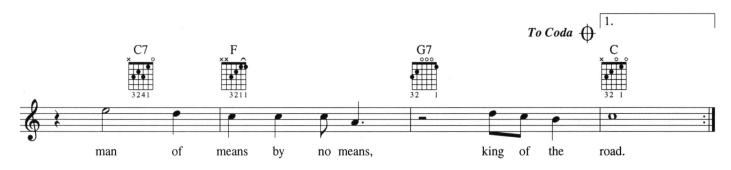

man of means by no means, king of the road.

2.   **Bridge**

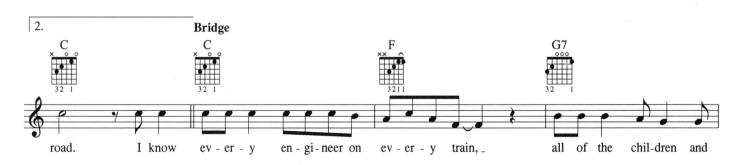

road. I know ev - er - y en - gi - neer on ev - er - y train, _ all of the chil - dren and

all of their names. _ And ev - er - y hand - out in ev - er - y town, _ and

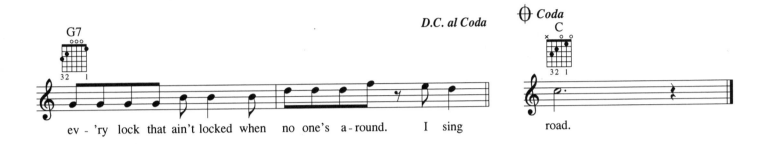

D.C. al Coda ⊕ *Coda*

ev - 'ry lock that ain't locked when no one's a - round. I sing road.

Additional Lyrics

2. Third box car, midnight train, destination: Bangor, Maine.
Old worn out suit and shoes; I don't pay no union dues.
I smoke old stogies I have found, short, but not too big around.
I'm a man of means by no means, king of the road.

Kiss an Angel Good Mornin'

Words and Music by Ben Peters

Strum Pattern: 5
Pick Pattern: 4

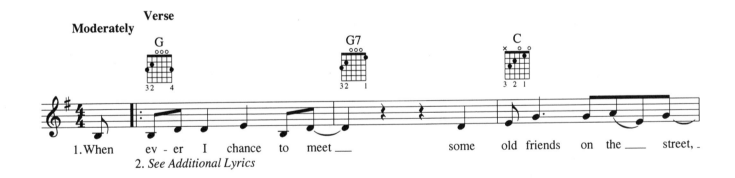

Moderately   **Verse**

1. When ev - er I chance to meet _ some old friends on the _ street, _
2. *See Additional Lyrics*

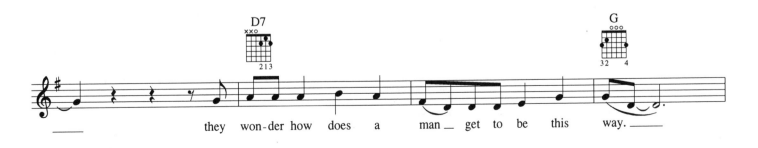

___ they won - der how does a man _ get to be this way. _

Additional Lyrics

2. Well people may try to guess the secret of happiness,
   But some of them never learn it's a simple thing.
   The secret I'm speakin' of is a woman and man in love,
   And the answer is in the song that I always sing.

Leavin' on Your Mind

Words and Music by Wayne P. Walker and Webb Pierce

Strum Pattern: 4
Pick Pattern: 2

Slowly

1. If you've got leav-in' on your mind, __ tell me now, get it o-ver. __ Hurt me now, get it

2., 3. See Additional Lyrics

o-ver, ___ if you've got leav-in' on your mind. 2. If there's a new love in your heart. __

Bridge

___ Don't leave me here in a world filled with dreams __ that might have been. Hurt me now, get it

o-ver. ___ I may learn to love a-gain. 3. If there's a new love in your

Coda

heart. ___ Hurt me now, get it o-ver. ___

If there's a new love in your heart. ___

Additional Lyrics

2., 3. If there's a new love in your heart,
Tell me now, get it over.
Hurt me now, get it over,
If there's a new love in your heart.

Living Proof

Words and Music by Johnny MacRae and Steve Clark

Strum Pattern: 4
Pick Pattern: 5

1. She hangs up the phone _____ and her heart starts to
2. *See Additional Lyrics*

pound. _____ Some-one just told _____ her an old friend's in _____

_____ town. _ And a mil-lion old feel - lin's come _ rush -

in' in, _____ start tear-in' to piec - es, what it took years _ to

Chorus

mend. _ She's liv - ing proof true love _____ nev-er

dies. _____ Through all of the heart - aches and all _____ the

good - byes. ___ She just can't for - get ___ it.

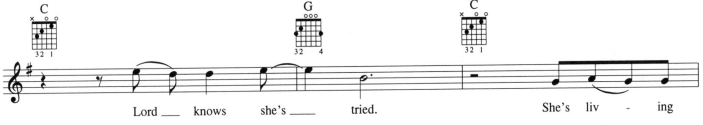

Lord ___ knows she's ___ tried. She's liv - ing

To Coda ⊕   *D.C. al Coda*

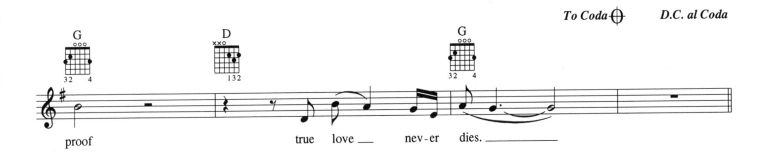

proof   true love ___ nev-er dies. ___

⊕ *Coda*

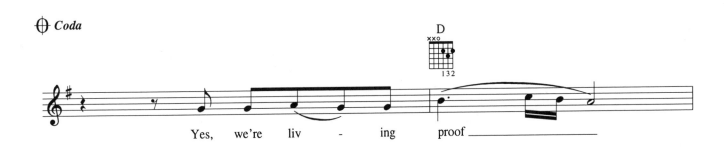

Yes,   we're liv - ing   proof ___

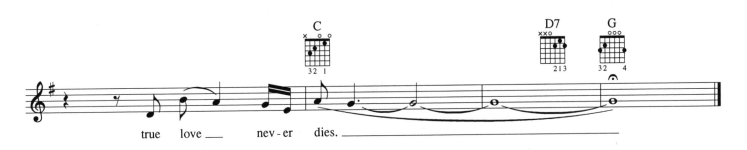

true love ___ nev - er dies. ___

Additional Lyrics

2. You answer the door and I say hello.
   If you don't want to see me just tell me, I'll go.
   But I can't live without you. It's only pretend.
   There's no love like your sweet love. Can we try it again?

Chorus We're living proof true love never dies.
          Through all of the heartache and all the goodbyes.
          I just can't forget you, Lord knows I've tried.
          We're living proof true love never dies.

Little Green Apples

Words and Music by Bobby Russell

Strum Pattern: 3
Pick Pattern: 3

2. Some -

Verse

times I call her up at home know-in' she's bus - y

and ask if she could get a - way and

meet me _____ and grab a bite to eat.

And she drops what she's do - in' and hur-ries down to meet me and I'm

al - ways late. But she sits wait-ing pa - tient - ly and

Repeat and Fade

smiles when she first sees me 'cause she's made that way.

The Long Black Veil

Words and Music by Marijohn Wilkin and Danny Dill

Strum Pattern: 4
Pick Pattern: 5

Additional Lyrics

2. The judge said, "Son, what is your alibi?
   If you were somewhere else, then you won't have to die."
   I spoke not a word although it meant my life.
   For I had been in the arms of my best friend's wife.

3. The scaffold was high and eternity near.
   She stood in the crowd and shed not a tear.
   But sometimes at night when the cold wind moans
   In a long black veil she cries o'er my bones.

Lookin' for Love

Words and Music by Wanda Mallette, Patti Ryan and Bob Morrison

Strum Pattern:4
Pick Pattern:5

Lucille

Words and Music by Roger Bowling and Hal Bynum

Strum Pattern: 7
Pick Pattern: 9

hun - gry ___ for laugh - ter ___ and here ev - er af - ter I'm af - ter what ev

- er the oth - er life brings." 2. In the turned to the

Chorus

wom - an and said, "You picked a fine time to leave ___ me Lu -

cile, with four hun - gry chil - dren and a crop in the

field. I've had ___ some bad times ___ lived through ___ some

sad times ___ but this time ___ your hurt - in' won't heal. You picked a

D.S. al Coda

fine time ___ to leave me Lu - cille."

Additional Lyrics

2. In the mirror I saw him and I closely watched him, I thought how he looked out of place.
   He came to the woman who sat down beside me, he had a strange look on his face.
   The big hands were calloused, he looked like a mountain, for a minute I thought I was dead.
   But he started shaking his big heart was breaking, he turned to the woman and said:

3. After he left us I ordered more whiskey I thought how she made him look small.
   From the lights of the bar room to a rented hotel room, we walked without talking at all.
   She was a beauty but when she came to me, she must have thought I've lost my mind;
   I couldn't hold her 'cause the words that he told her kept coming back time after time.

Luckenbach, Texas
(Back to the Basics of Love)

Words and Music by Bobby Emmons and Chips Moman

Strum Pattern: 3
Pick Pattern: 3

This coat and tie is cho-kin' me; ___ In your high so - ci - e - ty you

cry ___ all day. We've been so

bus - y keep - in' up with the Jones' ___ four car ga - rage, and we're

still build - in' on, may - be it's time ___ we got back to the

D.S. al Coda

ba - sics of love. ___ Let's go to

Coda

Out in Luck - en - bach, Tex - as, there ain't no - bod - y

feel - in' no pain. ___

Make the World Go Away

Words and Music by Hank Cochran

Strum Pattern: 1
Pick Pattern: 2

Additional Lyrics

2. I'm sorry if I hurt you,
   I'll make it up day by day.
   Just say you love me like you used to,
   And make the world go away.

Mama Tried

Words and Music by Merle Haggard

Strum Pattern: 3
Pick Pattern: 3

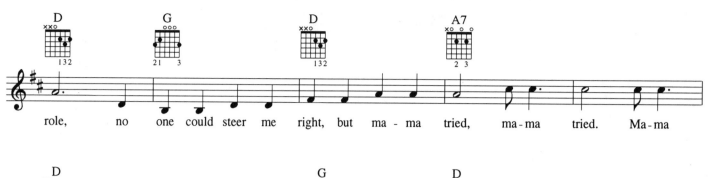

role, no one could steer me right, but ma-ma tried, ma-ma tried. Ma-ma

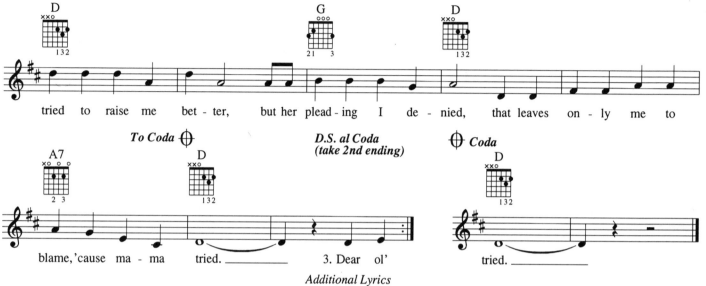

tried to raise me bet-ter, but her plead-ing I de-nied, that leaves on-ly me to

To Coda ⊕   *D.S. al Coda*   ⊕ *Coda*
               (take 2nd ending)

blame, 'cause ma-ma tried. _____ 3. Dear ol'   tried. _____

Additional Lyrics

2. One and only rebel child, from a fam'ly meek and mild,
   My mama seemed to know what lay in store.
   'Spite of all my Sunday learnin' t'wards the bad I kept turnin',
   'Til mama couldn't hold me anymore.

3. Dear ol' daddy, rest his soul, left my mom a heavy load.
   She tried so very hard to fill his shoes.
   Workin' hours without rest, wanted me to have the best,
   She tried to raise me right but I refused.

Rocky Top

Words and Music by Boudleaux Bryant and Felice Bryant

Strum Pattern: 4
Pick Pattern: 5

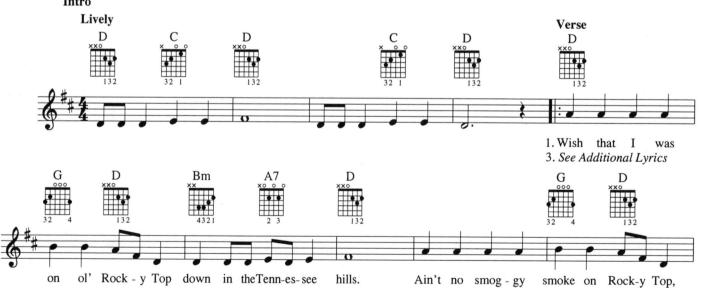

Intro
Lively

1. Wish that I was
3. *See Additional Lyrics*

on ol' Rock-y Top down in the Tenn-es-see hills.   Ain't no smog-gy smoke on Rock-y Top,

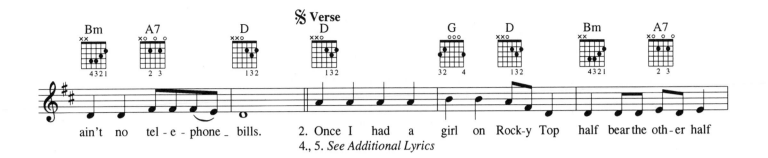

ain't no tel - e - phone _ bills.   2. Once I had a girl on Rock-y Top half bear the oth-er half
4., 5. *See Additional Lyrics*

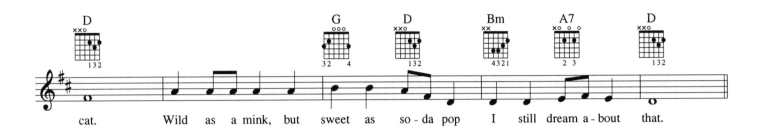

cat.   Wild as a mink, but sweet as so - da pop I still dream a - bout that.

Chorus

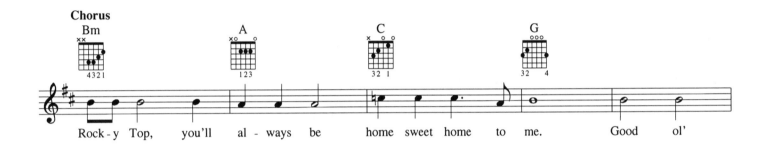

Rock - y Top,   you'll al - ways be   home sweet home to me.   Good ol'

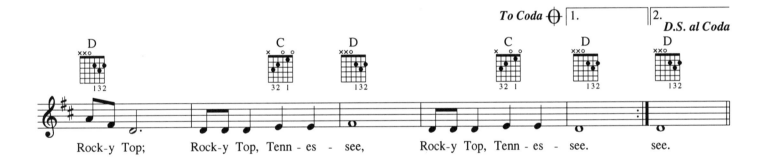

Rock - y Top;   Rock - y Top, Tenn - es - see,   Rock - y Top, Tenn - es - see.   see.

Coda

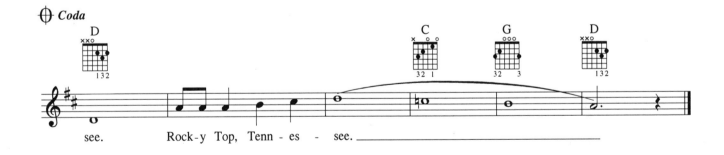

see.   Rock - y Top, Tenn - es - see. _____

Additional Lyrics

3. Once two strangers climbed ol' Rocky Top, lookin' for a moonshine still.
   Strangers ain't come down from Rocky Top, reckon they never will.

4. Corn won't grow at all on Rocky Top, dirt's too rocky by far.
   That's why all the folks on Rocky Top get their corn from a jar.

5. I've had years of cramped-up city life, trapped like a duck in a pen.
   All I know is it's a pity life can't be simple again.

Mammas Don't Let Your Babies Grow Up to Be Cowboys

Words and Music by Ed Bruce and Patsy Bruce

Strum Pattern: 8
Pick Pattern: 8

Verse

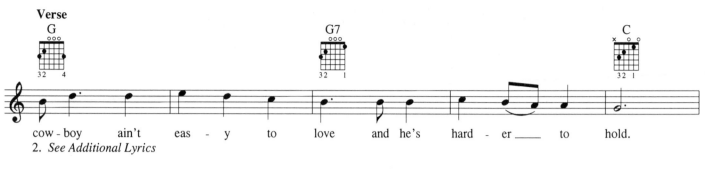

cow - boy ain't eas - y to love and he's hard - er ____ to hold.
2. *See Additional Lyrics*

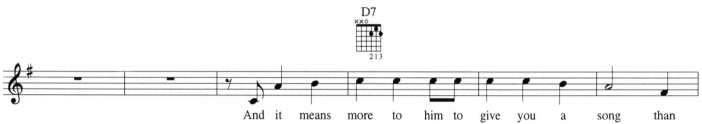

And it means more to him to give you a song than

sil - ver or gold. Bud - wei - ser

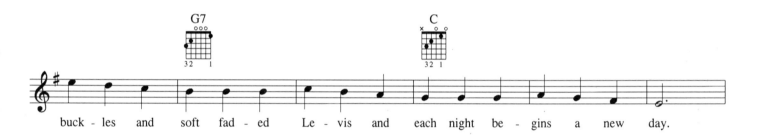

buck - les and soft fad - ed Le - vis and each night be - gins a new day.

If you can't un - der - stand ___ him ___ and he don't die ___ young, he'll prob - a - bly

just ride ___ a - way.

Additional Lyrics

2. A cowboy loves smoky ol' pool rooms and clear mountain mornings,
Little warm puppies and children and girls of the night.
Them that don't know him won't like him and
Them that do sometimes won't know how to take him.
He's not wrong, he's just different and his pride won't
Let him do things to make you think he's right.

Mississippi Woman

Words and Music by Red Lane

Strum Pattern: 4
Pick Pattern: 5

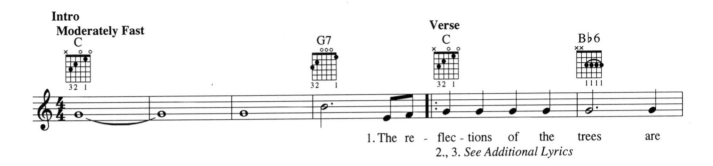

Intro
Moderately Fast

Verse

1. The re - flec - tions of the trees are
2., 3. *See Additional Lyrics*

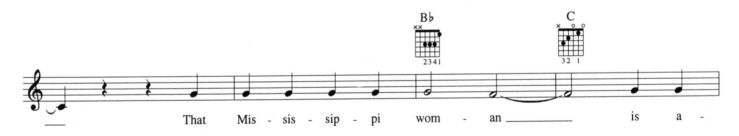

cut   by   the bow   of   my pi - rogue, _____   and

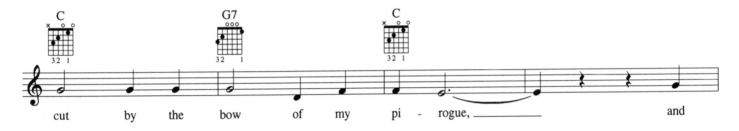

spat - tered   by   the pad - dle   of   my ea - ger   hand. ___

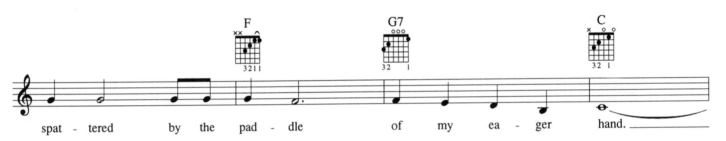

___   That   Mis - sis - sip - pi   wom - an _____   is   a -

wav - in'   o - ver   yon - der, _____   wav - in' her

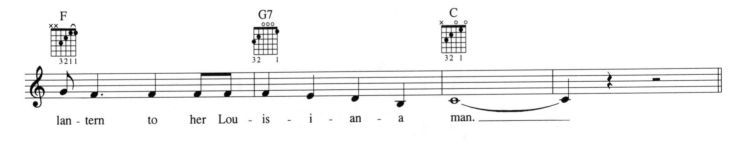

lan - tern   to   her Lou - is - i - an - a   man. ___

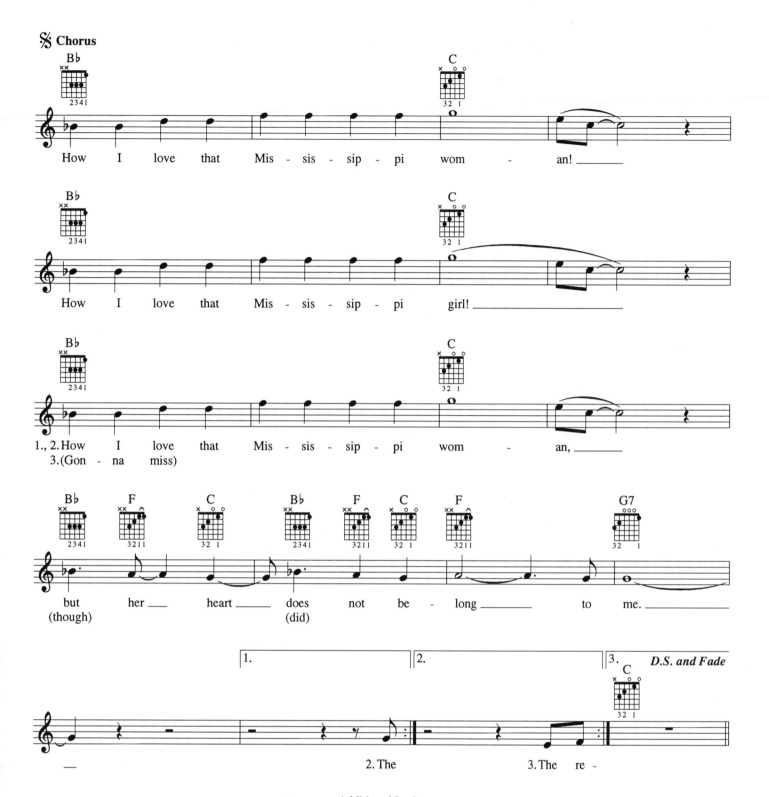

Additional Lyrics

2. The lantern light and moonbeams
   Are dancing patterns on the water.
   She doesn't seem to realize
   I've learned her secret plans.

   My jealous mind is thinking
   As I paddle through the sleepin' alligators.
   She don't know I know about her
   Louisiana man.

3. The reflections of the trees
   Are cut by the bow of my pirogue.
   And spattered by the paddle
   Of my shaky hand.

   The silence from behind me
   Is alive with splashing alligators,
   And the lantern light is blinking
   On the bottom of the sand.

My Heroes Have Always Been Cowboys

Words and Music by Sharon Vaughn

Strum Pattern: 9
Pick Pattern: 6

Verse
Moderately Slow

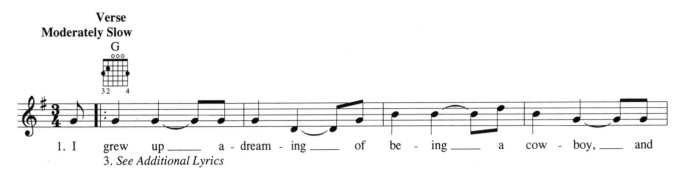

1. I grew up ___ a-dream-ing ___ of be-ing ___ a cow-boy, ___ and
3. *See Additional Lyrics*

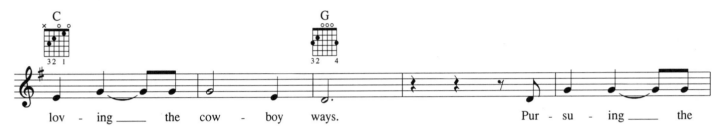

lov-ing ___ the cow-boy ways. Pur-su-ing ___ the

life of my high-rid-in' he-roes, ___ I burned up ___ my child-hood

days. 2. I learned all ___ the rules ___ of a mod-ern day
4. *See Additional Lyrics*

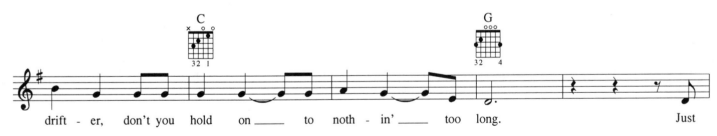

drift-er, don't you hold on ___ to noth-in' ___ too long. Just

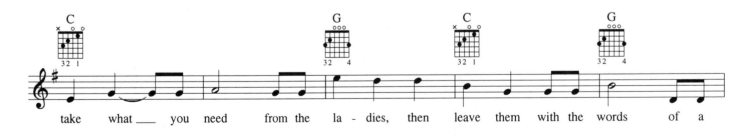

take what ___ you need from the la-dies, then leave them with the words of a

sad coun - try song.   My he - roes ___ have al - ways been

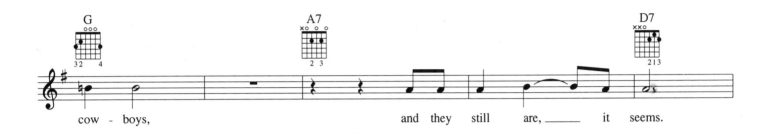

cow - boys,   and they still are, ___ it seems.

Sad - ly ___ in search of ___ and one step in back of ___ them -

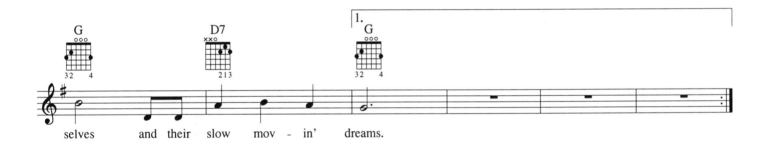

selves   and their slow mov - in' dreams.

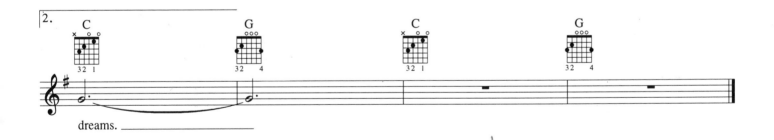

dreams. _____

Additional Lyrics

3. Cowboys are special with their own brand of mis'ry
   From being alone too long.
   You could die from the cold in the arms of a nightmare
   Knowing well that your best days are gone.

4. Pickin' up hookers instead of my pen,
   I let the words of my youth fade away.
   Old worn out saddles and old worn out mem'ries
   With no one and no place to stay.

Night Life

Words and Music by Willie Nelson, Walt Breeland and Paul Buskirk

Strum Pattern: 3
Pick Pattern: 3

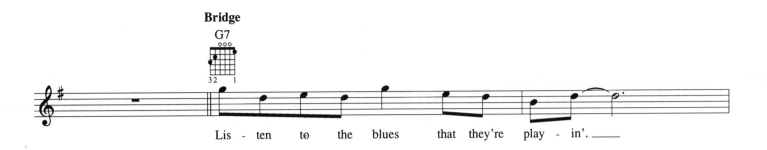

Bridge

Lis - ten to the blues that they're play - in'. ____

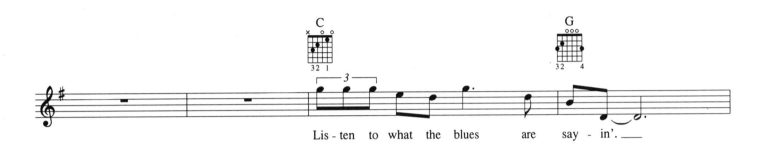

Lis - ten to what the blues are say - in'. ____

3., 6. My, it's just ____ an - oth - er scene from the

world ____ of bro - ken dreams. The night life ____ ain't a good life, ___ but it's

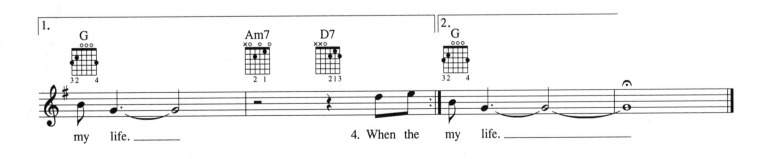

1.
my life. ____

2.
4. When the my life. ____

115

My Elusive Dreams

Words and Music by Curly Putman and Billy Sherrill

Strum Pattern: 4
Pick Pattern: 5

Additional Lyrics

2. You had my child in Memphis, I heard of work in Nashville,
We didn't find it there so we moved on.
To a small farm in Nebraska to a gold mine in Alaska,
We didn't find it there so we moved on.

3. And now we've left Alaska because there was no gold mine,
But this time only two of us move on.
Now all we have is each other and a little memory to cling to,
And still you won't let me go on alone.

Okie from Muskogee

Words and Music by Merle Haggard and Roy Edward Burris

Strum Pattern: 4
Pick Pattern: 5

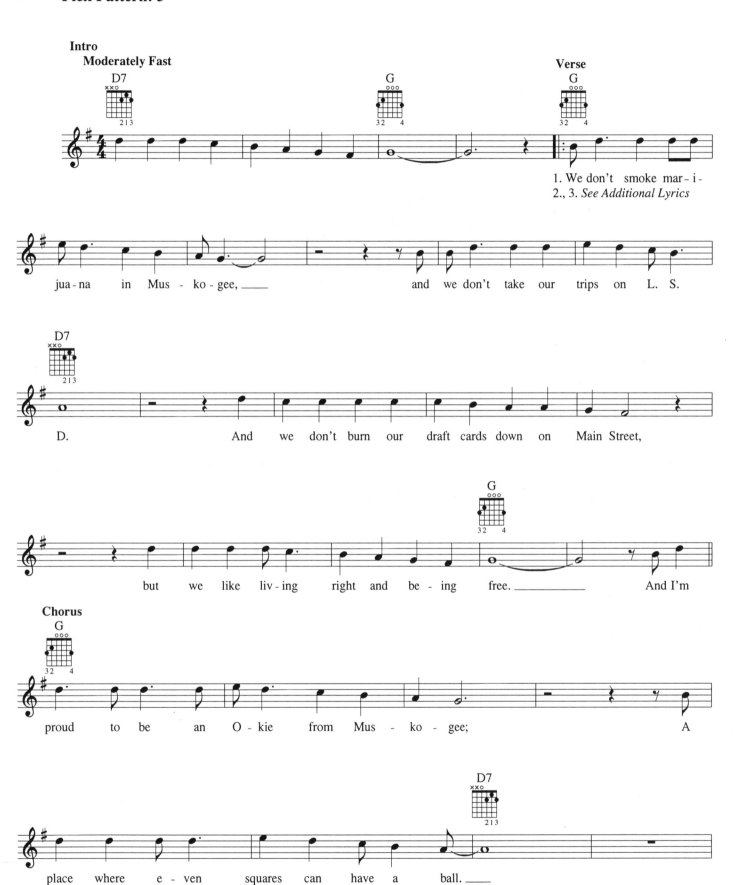

We still wave Ol' Glo-ry down at the court house, white light-ning's still the

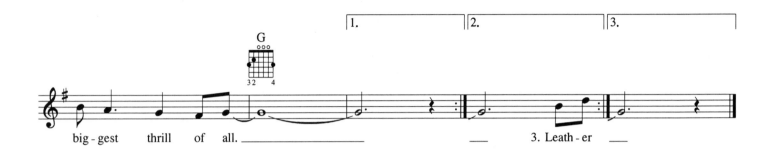

1. 2. 3.

big-gest thrill of all. _____ ___ 3. Leath-er ___

Additional Lyrics

2. We don't make a party out of loving,
   But we like holding hands and pitching woo.
   We don't let our hair grow long and shaggy,
   Like the hippies out in San Francisco do.

3. Leather boots are still in style if a man needs footwear.
   Beads and Roman sandals won't be seen.
   Football's still the roughest thing on campus,
   And the kids here still respect the college dean.

Older Women

Words and Music by Jamie O'Hara

Strum Pattern: 2
Pick Pattern: 4

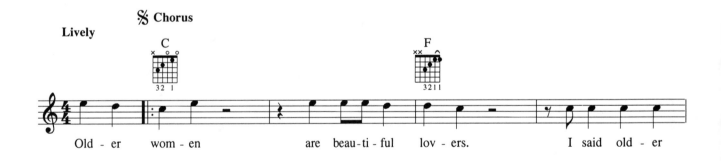

𝄋 **Chorus**

Lively

Old-er wom-en are beau-ti-ful lov-ers. I said old-er

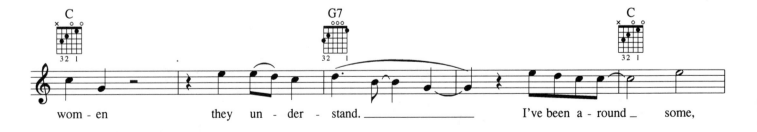

wom-en they un-der-stand. _____ I've been a-round_ some,

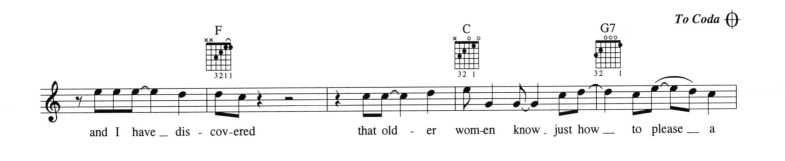

and I have — dis - cov-ered   that old - er wom-en know — just how — to please — a

Verse

man.   1. Ev - 'ry - bod - y   seems to love those
2. *See Additional Lyrics*

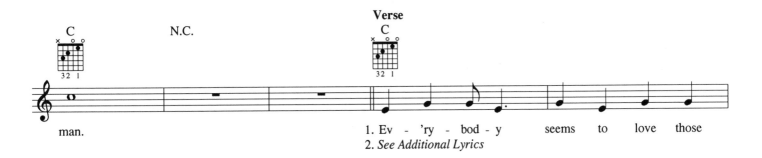

young - er wom-en,   from eight - een   on   up   to twen - ty - five. —

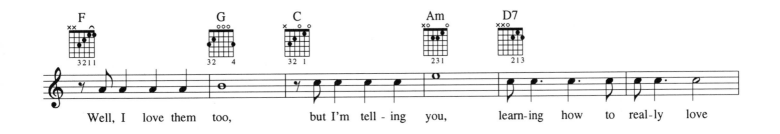

Well, I love them too,   but I'm tell - ing   you,   learn-ing how   to real-ly love

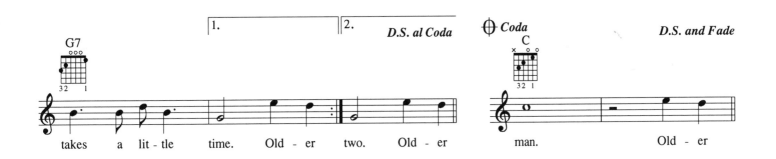

1.   **2.**   *D.S. al Coda*   ⊕ *Coda*   *D.S. and Fade*

takes   a   lit - tle   time. Old - er two. Old - er   man.   Old - er

Additional Lyrics

2. So baby, don't you worry about growing older.
   Those young girls, they've got nothing on you.
   'Cause it takes some living, to get good at giving,
   And giving love is just where you could teach them a thing or two.

Old Dogs, Children and Watermelon Wine

Words and Music by Tom T. Hall

Strum Pattern: 2
Pick Pattern: 4

Intro
Moderately

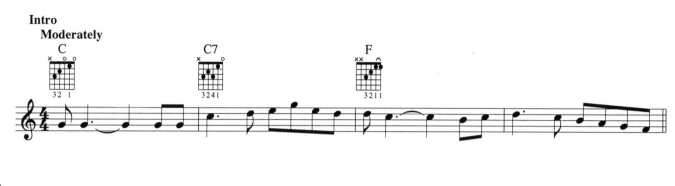

Verse

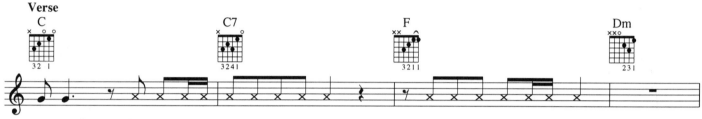

Spoken: 1. How old do you think I am, he said.   I said well I did-n't know.

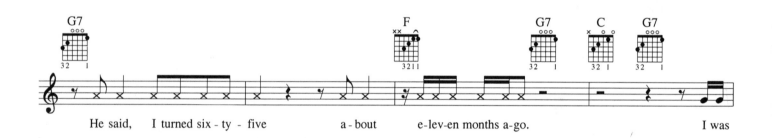

He said,   I turned six - ty - five   a - bout   e-lev-en months a-go.   I was

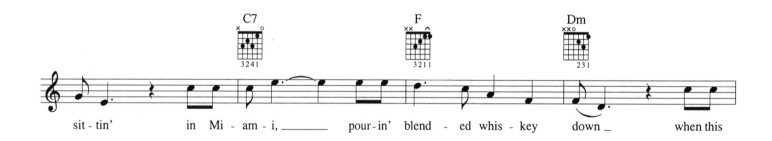

sit - tin'   in Mi - am - i, _____ pour-in' blend - ed whis - key   down _   when this

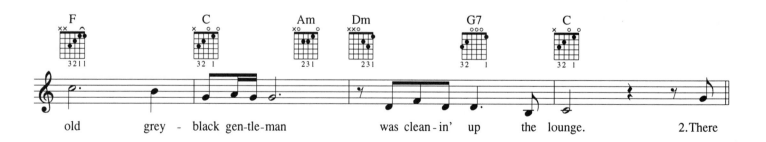

old   grey - black gen-tle-man   was clean - in' up   the lounge.   2. There

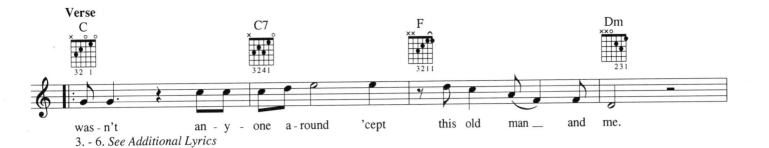

was-n't an - y - one a - round 'cept this old man ___ and me.

3. - 6. *See Additional Lyrics*

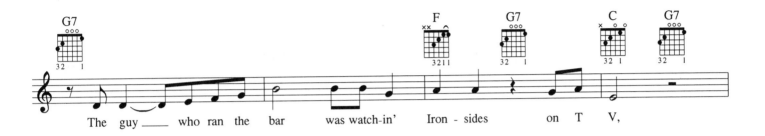

The guy ___ who ran the bar was watch-in' Iron - sides on T V,

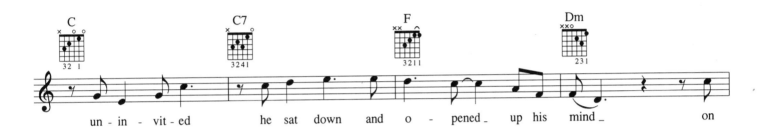

un - in - vit - ed he sat down and o - pened ___ up his mind ___ on

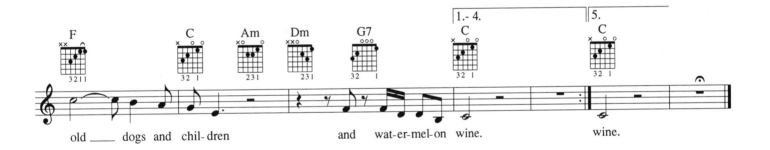

old ___ dogs and chil-dren and wat-er-mel-on wine. wine.

Additional Lyrics

3. Ever had a drink of watermelon wine? He asked.
   He told me all about it though I didn't answer back.
   Ain't but three things in this world that's worth a solitary dime,
   But old dogs, children and watermelon wine.

4. He said women think about theyselves when menfolk ain't around,
   And friends are hard to find when they discover that you down.
   He said I tried it all when I was young and in my natural prime;
   Now it's old dogs, children and watermelon wine.

5. Old dogs care about you even when you make mistakes.
   God bless little children while they're still too young to hate.
   When he moved away, I found my pen and copied down that line,
   'Bout old dogs and children and watermelon wine.

6. I had to catch a plane to Atlanta that next day.
   As I left for my room I saw him pickin' up my change.
   That night I dreamed in peaceful sleep of shady summertime,
   Of old dogs and children and watermelon wine.

Paper Roses

Words by Janice Torre   Music By Fred Spielman

Strum Pattern: 4
Pick Pattern: 5

Additional Lyrics

Boy 2. Your pretty lips look so warm and appealing;
They seem to have the sweetness of a rose;
But when you give a kiss there is no feeling;
It's just a stiff and artificial pose.

Girl 3. I thought that you would be a perfect lover.
You seemed so full of sweetness at the start.
But like a big red rose that's made of paper,
There isn't any sweetness in your heart.

Pick Me Up on Your Way Down

Words and Music by Harlan Howard

Strum Pattern: 5
Pick Pattern: 3

1. You were

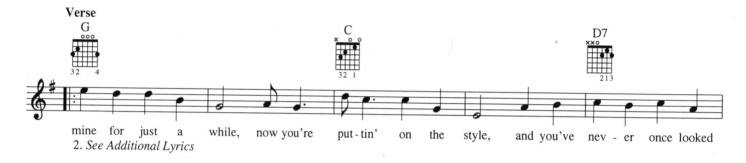

mine for just a while, now you're put-tin' on the style, and you've nev-er once looked
2. *See Additional Lyrics*

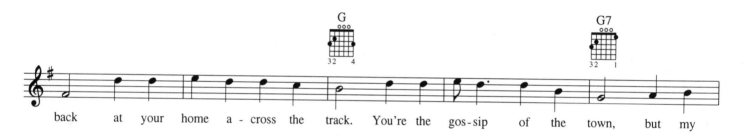

back at your home a-cross the track. You're the gos-sip of the town, but my

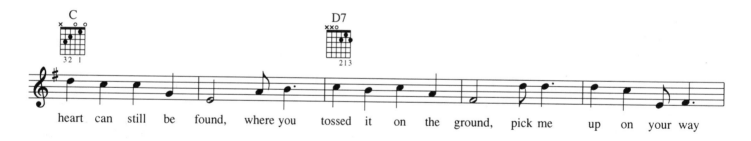

heart can still be found, where you tossed it on the ground, pick me up on your way

down. _____ Pick me up on your way down. When you're blue and all a-

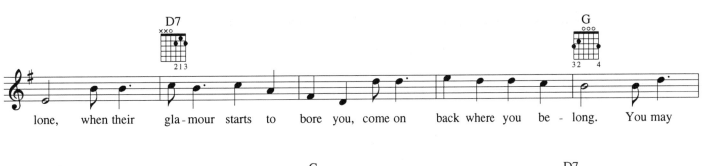

lone, when their gla-mour starts to bore you, come on back where you be - long. You may

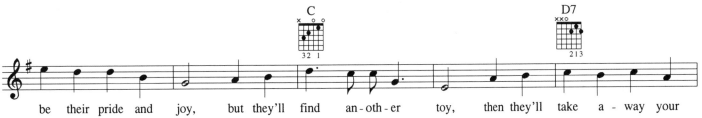

be their pride and joy, but they'll find an-oth-er toy, then they'll take a - way your

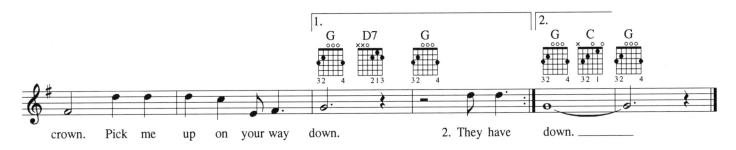

crown. Pick me up on your way down.   2. They have down. ____

Additional Lyrics

2. They have changed your attitude, made you haughty and so rude.
   Your new friends can take the blame, underneath you're still the same.
   When you learn these things are true, I'll be waiting here for you.
   As you tumble to the ground, pick me up on your way down.

She's Got You

Words and Music by Hank Cochran

Strum Pattern: 1
Pick Pattern: 2

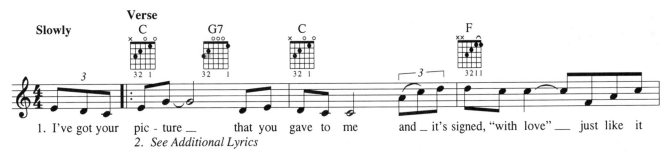

1. I've got your pic - ture ___ that you gave to me and ___ it's signed, "with love" ___ just like it
2. *See Additional Lyrics*

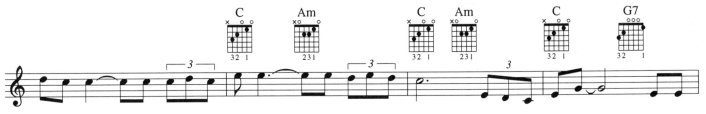

used to be. ___ The on - ly thing dif - f'rent, ___ the on - ly thing new,   I've got your pic - ture, ___ she's got

you.   2. I've got the   you.   I've got your mem-o-ry, ___ or has it got   me? ___   I real-ly don't

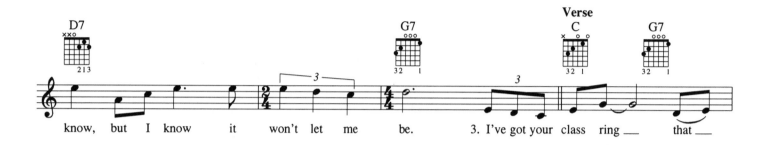

know,   but   I   know   it   won't let   me   be.   3. I've got your class ring ___   that ___

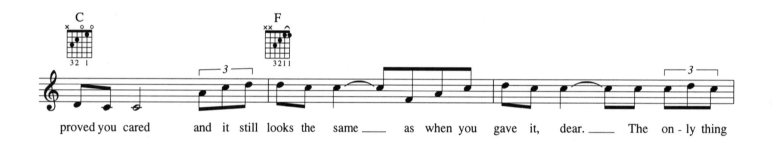

proved you cared   and it still looks the   same ___ as when you   gave it,   dear. ___ The on-ly thing

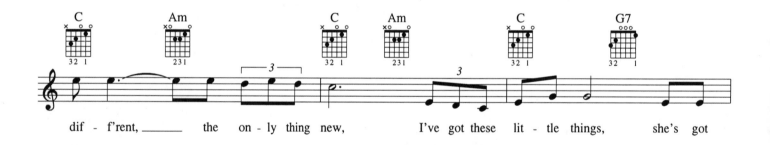

dif - f'rent, ___ the   on-ly thing new,   I've got these lit-tle things,   she's got

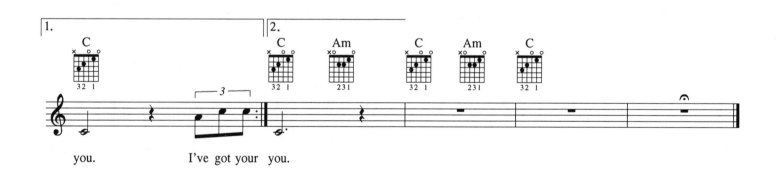

you.   I've got your you.

Additional Lyrics

2. I've got the records that we used to share,
And they still sound the same as when you were here.
The only thing diff'rent, the only thing new,
I've got the records, she's got you.

Room Full of Roses

Words and Music by Tim Spencer

Strum Pattern: 4
Pick Pattern: 5

(I'm A) Ramblin' Man

Words and Music by Ray Pennington

Strum Pattern: 4
Pick Pattern: 5

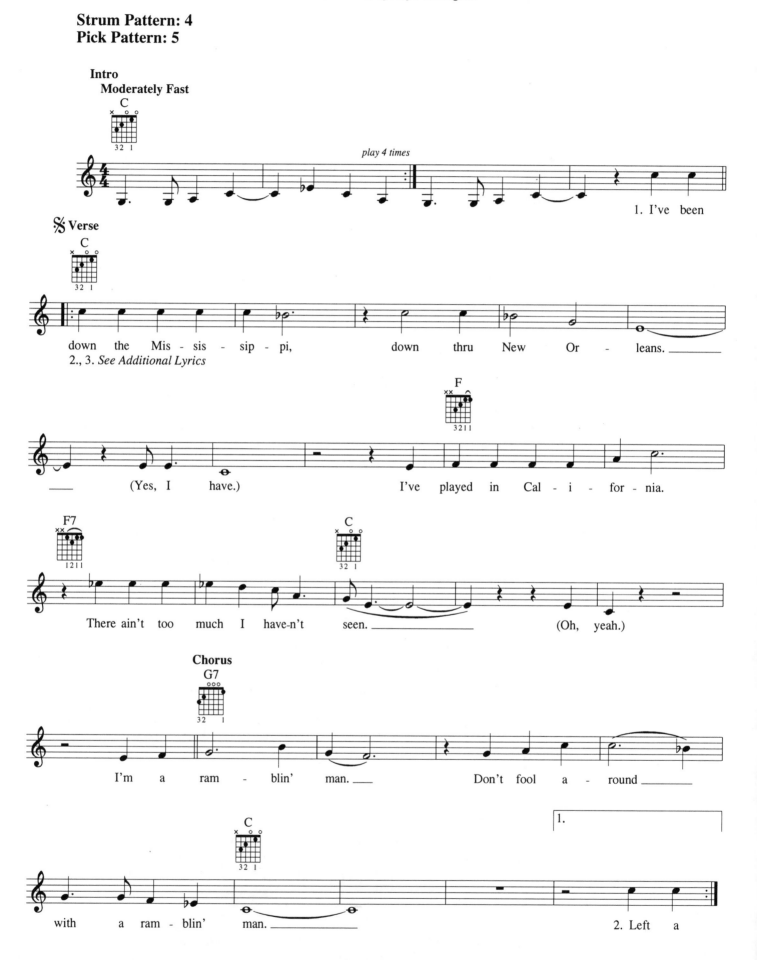

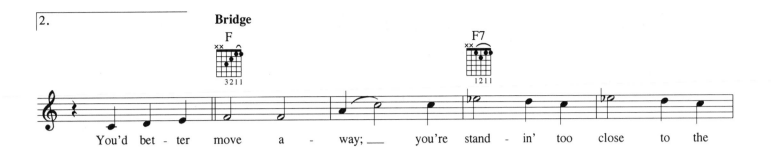

Bridge

You'd bet - ter move a - way; ___ you're stand - in' too close to the

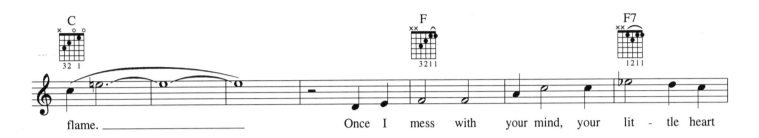

flame. _____ Once I mess with your mind, your lit - tle heart

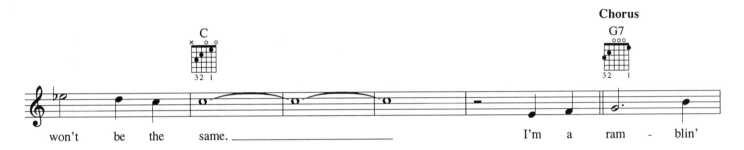

Chorus

won't be the same. _____ I'm a ram - blin'

To Coda ⊕

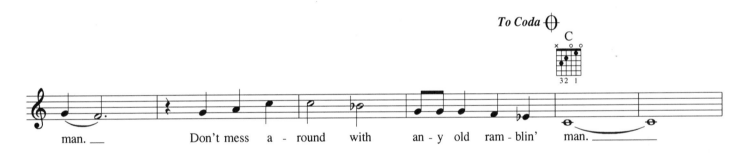

man. _ Don't mess a - round with an - y old ram - blin' man. _____

⊕ *Coda*

Repeat and Fade

D.S. al Coda
(take 2nd ending)

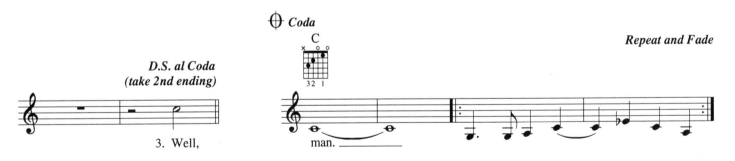

3. Well,   man. _____

Addtional Lyrics

2. Left a girl in West Virginia, up there where the green grass grows.
   (Yes, I did.)
   Got a girl in Cincinnati waitin' where the Ohio River flows.
   (Oh, girl.)

Chorus   I'm a ramblin' man. Don't give your heart
          To a ramblin' man.

3. Well, up in Chicago I was known as quite a boy.
   (Yes, I was.)
   Down in Alabama they call me the man of joy.
   (Still do.)

Chorus: I'm a ramblin' man. Don't fall in love
          With a ramblin' man.

Ruby, Don't Take Your Love to Town

Words and Music by Mel Tillis

Strum Pattern: 4
Pick Pattern: 5

1. You have paint-ed up your lips and rolled and curled your tint-ed hair.
2., 3. *See Additional Lyrics*

Ru - by are you con-tem-plat-ing go-ing out some-where? The sha-dows on the wall tell me the sun is go-ing down. Oh,

To Coda

Ru - by, don't take your love to

Chorus

town. For it was-n't me that start-ed that old cra-zy As-ia war, but I was proud to go and do my pa-tri-ot-ic

Oh, I know, Ru-by, that I'm not the man I used to

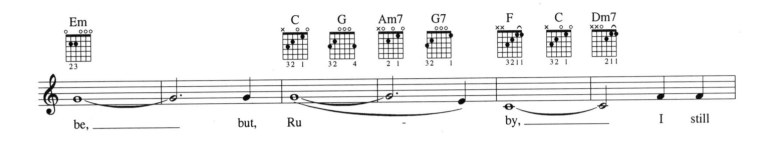

be, _____ but, Ru - by, _____ I still

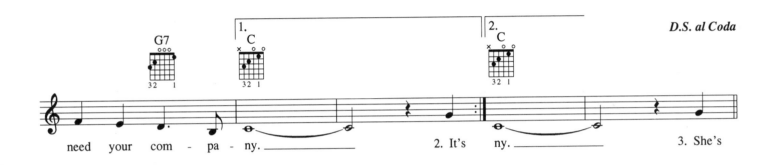

D.S. al Coda

need your com - pa - ny. _____ 2. It's ny. _____ 3. She's

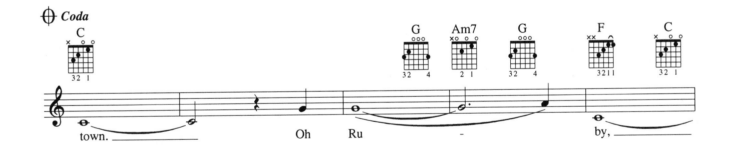

town. _____ Oh Ru - by, _____

Spoken: For God's sake, turn a - round.

Addtional Lyrics

1. It's hard to love a man whose legs are bent and paralyzed,
   And the wants and need of a woman your age Ruby, I realize.
   But it won't be long, I've heard them say until I'm not around.
   Oh, Ruby, don't take your love to town.

3. She's leaving now 'cause I just heard the slamming of the door.
   The way I know I've heard it slam one hundred times before,
   And if I could move I'd get my gun and put her in the ground.
   Oh, Ruby, don't take your love to town.

Saginaw, Michigan

Words and Music by Don Wayne and Bill Anderson

Strum Pattern:4
Pick Pattern:5

Intro
Moderately Fast

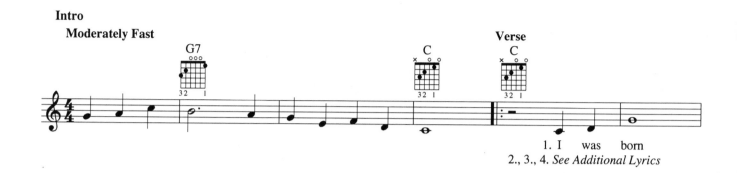

1. I was born
2., 3., 4. *See Additional Lyrics*

in Sag - i - naw, Mich - i - gan. _____ I grew up in a house on Sag - i - naw

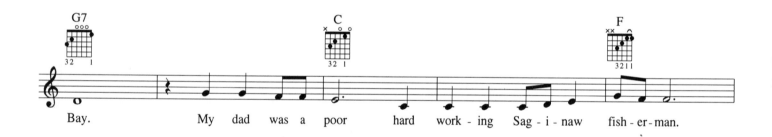

Bay. My dad was a poor hard work - ing Sag - i - naw fish - er - man.

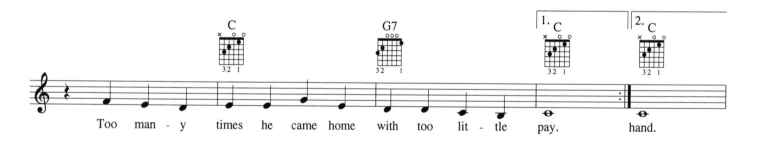

Too man - y times he came home with too lit - tle pay. hand.

Bridge

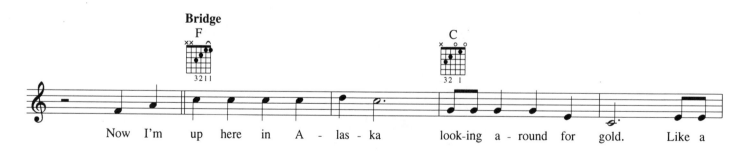

Now I'm up here in A - las - ka look-ing a - round for gold. Like a

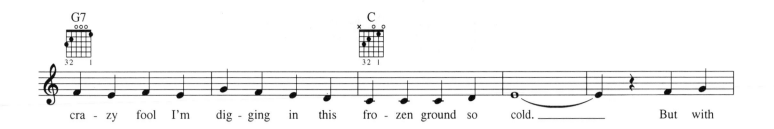

cra - zy fool I'm dig - ging in this fro - zen ground so cold. _____ But with

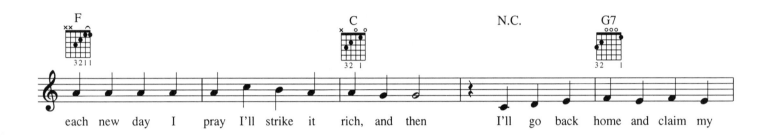

each new day I pray I'll strike it rich, and then I'll go back home and claim my

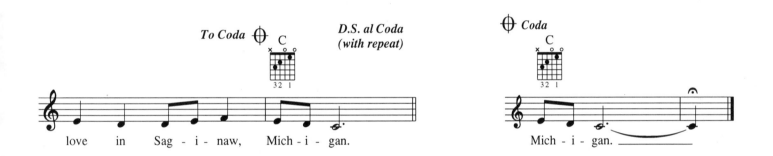

To Coda ⊕

D.S. al Coda
(with repeat)

⊕ *Coda*

love in Sag - i - naw, Mich - i - gan.

Mich - i - gan. _____

Additional Lyrics

2. I loved a girl in Saginaw, Michigan,
   The daughter of a wealthy man.
   But he called me that son of a Saginaw fisherman,
   Not good enough to claim his daughter's hand.

3. I wrote my love in Saginaw, Michigan.
   I said, "Honey, I'm coming home, please wait for me.
   You can tell your dad I'm coming back a richer man.
   I hit the biggest strike in Klondike history."

4. Her dad met me in Saginaw, Michigan.
   He gave me a great big party with champagne.
   Then he said, "Son, you're a wise, young ambitious man.
   Will you sell your father-in-law your Klondike claim?"

Bridge   Now he's up there in Alaska digging in the cold, cold ground.
           The greedy fool is looking for the gold I never found.
           It serves him right and no one here is missing him,
           Least of all the newlyweds of Saginaw, Michigan.

Satin Sheets

Words and Music by John E. Volinkaty

Strum Pattern: 3
Pick Pattern: 3

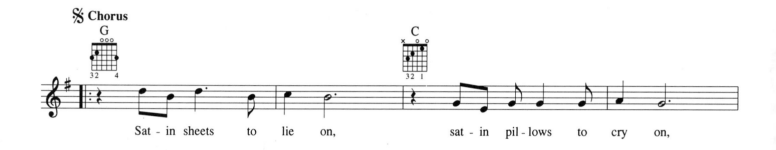

Sat - in sheets to lie on, sat - in pil - lows to cry on,

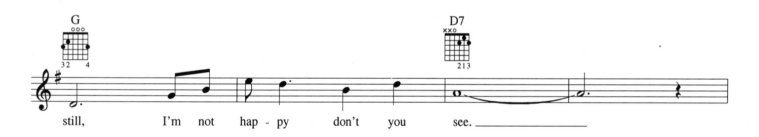

still, I'm not hap - py don't you see. _____

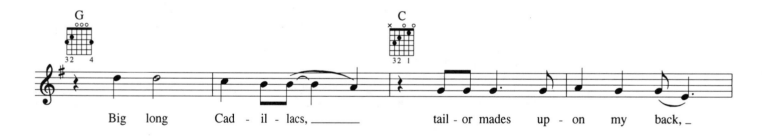

Big long Cad - il - lacs, _____ tail - or mades up - on my back, _

To Coda

still, I want you to set _____ me free. _____

MCA music publishing

Verse

1. I've found an-oth-er man _____ who can give more than you can, _ though you've
2., 3. *See Additional Lyrics*

giv - en me ev - 'ry - thing mon - ey can buy. _____

But your mon - ey can't hold me tight _ like he does ____ on a long, long night. _

1., 2.

You know ____ you did - n't keep me sat - is - fied. _____

3.

D.S. al Coda Coda

eyes. _____ ____

Additional Lyrics

2. We've been through thick and thin together
Braved the fair and stormy weather.
We've had all the hard times, you and I.
And now that I'm a big success
You called today and you confessed
And told me things that made me want to die.

3. You told me there's another woman
Who can give you more than I can
And I've given ev'rything that cash will buy.
You can't buy me a peaceful night
With loving arms around me tight
And you're too busy to notice the hurt in my eyes.

Sixteen Tons

Words and Music by Merle Travis

Strum Pattern: 4
Pick Pattern: 5

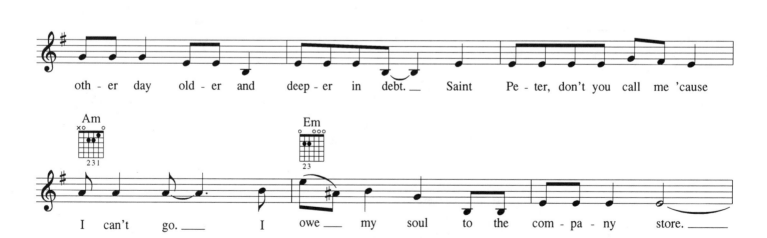

2. I was

Additional Lyrics

2. I was born one mornin' when the sun didn't shine.
   I picked up my shovel and I walked to the mine.
   I loaded sixteen tons of number nine coal,
   And the straw boss said, "Well a bless my soul." You load,

3. I was born one mornin'; it was drizzling rain.
   Fightin' and trouble are my middle name.
   I was raised in a cane brake by an ole mama lion,
   Cain't no high toned woman make me walk the line. You load,

4 If you see me comin' better step aside,
   A lotta men didn't; a lotta men died.
   One fist of iron the other of steel,
   If the right don't get you, then the left one will. You load,

Some Days Are Diamonds
(Some Days Are Stone)

Words and Music by Dick Feller

Strum Pattern: 1
Pick Pattern: 2

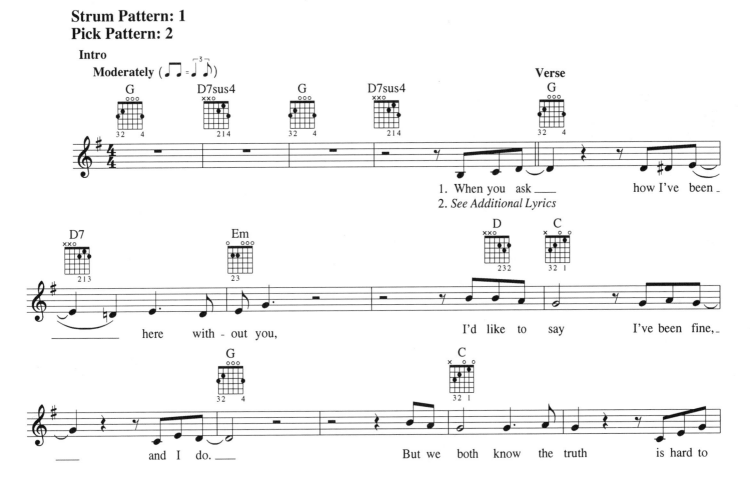

1. When you ask _____ how I've been _____
2. *See Additional Lyrics*

here with - out you, I'd like to say I've been fine,_

_____ and I do. _____ But we both know the truth is hard to

Additional Lyrics

2. Now the face that I see in my mirror,
More and more, is a stranger to me.
More and more, I can see there's a danger
In becoming what I never thought I'd be.

She Believes in Me

Words and Music by Steve Gibb

Strum Pattern: 4
Pick Pattern: 5

hold her tight. _ And she be-lieves in me. I'll nev-er know just what she

sees in me. ___ I told her some-day if she was my girl _____ I could

change _ the world _ with my lit-tle songs, _____ I was wrong. But she has

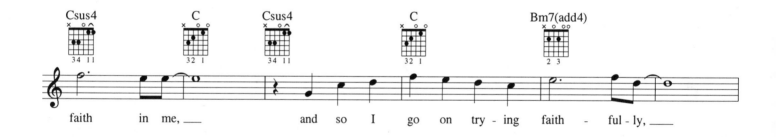

faith in me, ___ and so I go on try-ing faith - ful-ly, ___

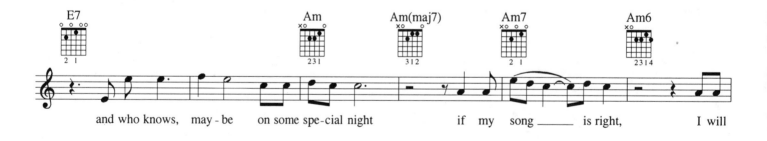

and who knows, may-be on some spe-cial night if my song _____ is right, I will

find a way, _ find a way. 3. While she lays wait-ing I

stum-ble to the kit-chen for a bite. _____ Then I see my old gui-tar in _____ the

night, just wait-ing for me like _____ a sec-ret friend, and there's no

end. While she lays cry-ing I fum-ble with a mel - o - dy or _____

two, then I'm torn be-tween the things that I should do. Then she

D.S. al Coda

says to wake her up _____ when I am through. *Spoken:* God, her love is true.

⊕ Coda

While she waits.

While _____ she waits _____ for me. _____

Son-of-a-Preacher Man

Words and Music by John Hurley and Ronnie Wilkins

Strum Pattern: 2
Pick Pattern: 4

Additional Lyrics

2. Being good isn't always easy no matter how I try.
When he started sweet talkin' to me he'd come and tell me ev'rything is alright;
Kiss and tell me ev'rything is alright, and "Can I sneak away again tonight."
Lord knows to my surprise,

(I'm A) Stand by My Woman Man

Words and Music by Kent Robbins

Strum Pattern: 4
Pick Pattern: 5

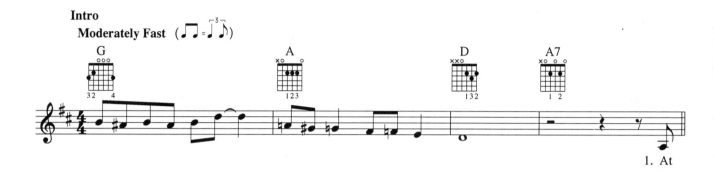

1. At

five o' clock she knows ____ I'll soon be home. ____
2. *See Additional Lyrics*

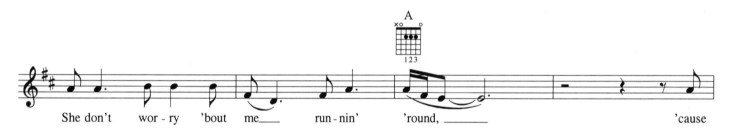

She don't wor-ry 'bout me ____ run-nin' 'round, ____ 'cause

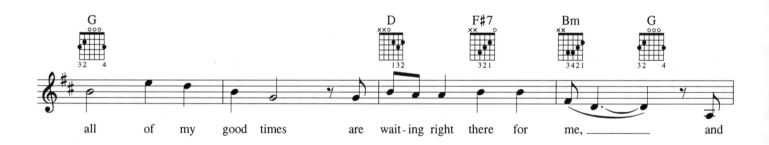

all of my good times are wait-ing right there for me, ____ and

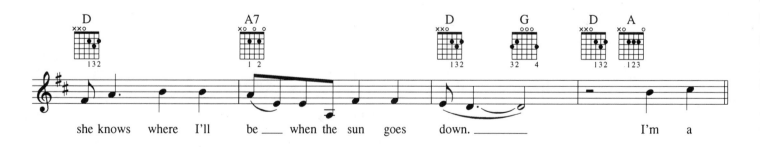

she knows where I'll be ____ when the sun goes down. ____ I'm a

stand by my wom-an man. ___ Our world turns ___ a-round a lit-tle gold band, _____ and

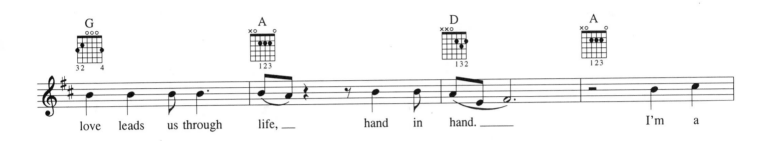

love leads us through life, ___ hand in hand. _____ I'm a

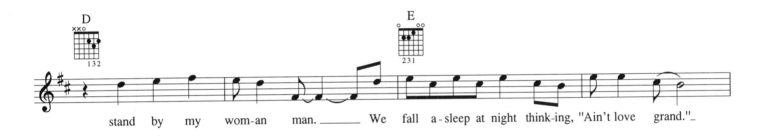

stand by my wom-an man. _____ We fall a-sleep at night think-ing, "Ain't love grand."_

To Coda ⊕   1.   2.   *D.S. al Coda*

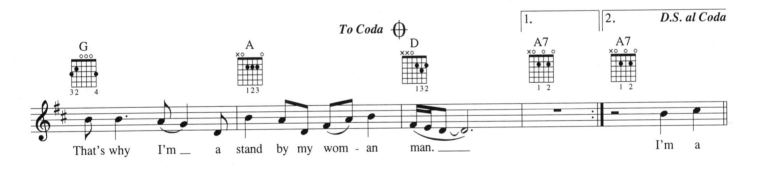

That's why I'm ___ a stand by my wom-an man. _____   I'm a

⊕ *Coda*

man. ___ That's why I'm ___ a stand by my wom-an man. ___

Additional Lyrics

2. When she's down, she knows I'll be beside her,
   'Cause I'm not just her lover, I'm her friend.
   Our love keeps getting better and I'll gladly spend forever
   Standing by the woman who stands by her man.

Streets of Bakersfield

Words and Music by Homer Joy

Strum Pattern: 4
Pick Pattern: 5

Intro
Brightly

1. I came here look-ing for
3. *See Additional Lyrics*

Verse

some - thing _____ I could-n't find an-y-where else. _____

Hey, I'm not tryin' to be no-bod-y, I just want a

chance to be __ my self.

2. I've spent a thou-sand miles of
4. *See Additional Lyrics*

Verse

thumb - ing. _ Yes, I've worn blis-ters on __ my heels, _

Additional Lyrics

3. I spent some time in San Francisco.
   I spent a night there in the can.
   They threw this drunk man in my jail cell.
   I took fifteen dollars from that man.

4. Left him my watch and my old house key.
   Don't want folks thinkin' that I'd steal.
   Then I thanked him as I was leaving,
   And I headed out for Bakersfield.

Sunday Mornin' Comin' Down

Words and Music by Kris Kristofferson

Strum Pattern: 1
Pick Pattern: 2

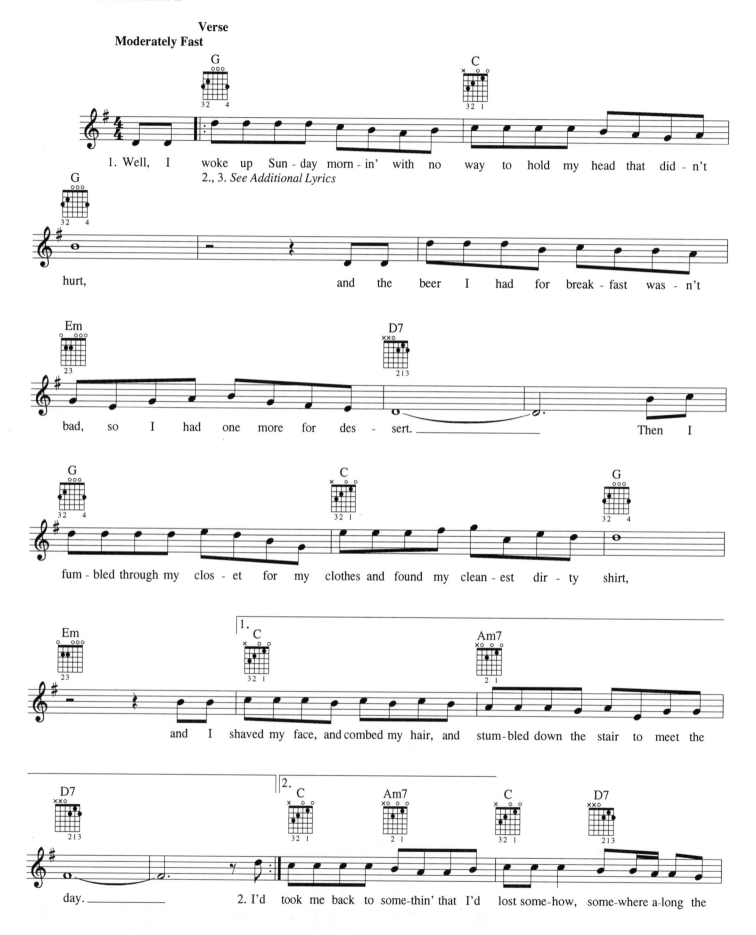

Verse
Moderately Fast

1. Well, I woke up Sun-day morn-in' with no way to hold my head that did-n't
2., 3. *See Additional Lyrics*

hurt, and the beer I had for break-fast was-n't

bad, so I had one more for des - sert. _____ Then I

fum-bled through my clos-et for my clothes and found my clean-est dir-ty shirt,

1. and I shaved my face, and combed my hair, and stum-bled down the stair to meet the

2. day. _____ 2. I'd took me back to some-thin' that I'd lost some-how, some-where a-long the

Chorus

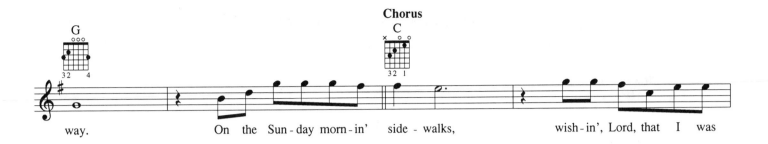

way. On the Sun-day morn-in' side-walks, wish-in', Lord, that I was

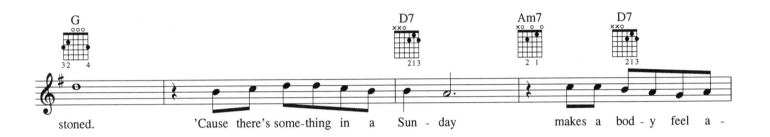

stoned. 'Cause there's some-thing in a Sun - day makes a bod-y feel a -

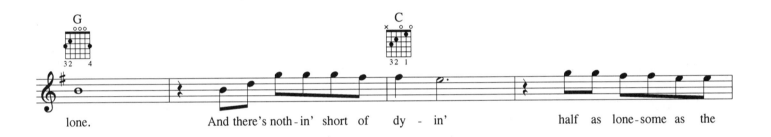

lone. And there's noth-in' short of dy - in' half as lone-some as the

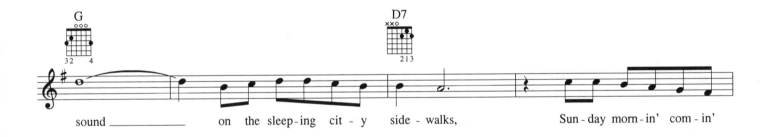

sound _____ on the sleep-ing cit - y side - walks, Sun - day morn-in' com-in'

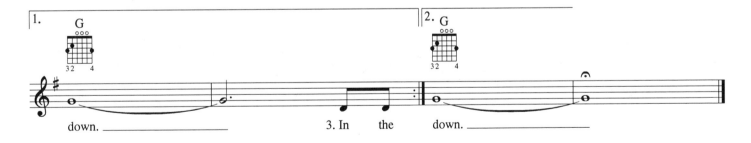

1. G
down. _____

2. G
3. In the down. _____

Additional Lyrics

2. I'd smoked my brain the night before with cigarettes and song that I'd been pickin'.
   But I lit my first and watched a small kid cussin' at a can that he was kickin'.
   Then I crossed the empty street and caught the Sunday smell of someone fryin' chicken,
   And it took me back to somethin' that I'd lost somehow, somewhere along the way.

3. In the park I saw a daddy with a laughing little girl that he was swingin',
   And I stopped beside a Sunday school and listened to the song that they were singin'.
   Then I headed back for home, and somewhere far away a lonely bell was ringin',
   And it echoed thru the canyon like the disappearing dreams of yesterday.

Tennessee Flat Top Box

Words and Music by Johnny Cash

Strum Pattern: 2
Pick Pattern: 4

1. In a lit - tle cab - a - ret in a South Tex - as
2., 3. *See Additional Lyrics*

bor - der - town, __ sat a boy and his gui - tar, ___ and the peo - ple came from

all a - round. __ And all the girls _____ from there to

Aus - tin ___ were slip - ping a - way __ from home and put - ting

jewel - ry in hock __ to take __ a trip to go and

lis - ten to the lit - tle dark - haired boy who played the Ten - nes - see flat top box. And he would play.

Interlude

1., 2.

3.

Repeat and Fade

Additional Lyrics

2. Well, he couldn't ride or wrangle and he never cared to make a dime,
   But give him his guitar, and he'd be happy all the time.
   And all the girls from nine to ninety
   Were snapping fingers, tapping toes and begging him, "Don't stop,"
   And hypnotized, and fascinated by the
   Little dark haired boy who played Tennessee flat top box.
   And he would play.

3. Then one day he was gone and no one ever saw him 'round.
   He vanished like the breeze; they forgot him in the little town.
   But all the girls still dreamed about him.
   And hung around the cabaret until the doors were locked.
   And then one day on the hit parade was a
   Little dark haired boy who played Tennessee flat top box.
   And he would play.

The Vows Go Unbroken
(Always True to You)

Words and Music by Gary Burr and Eric Kaz

MCA music publishing

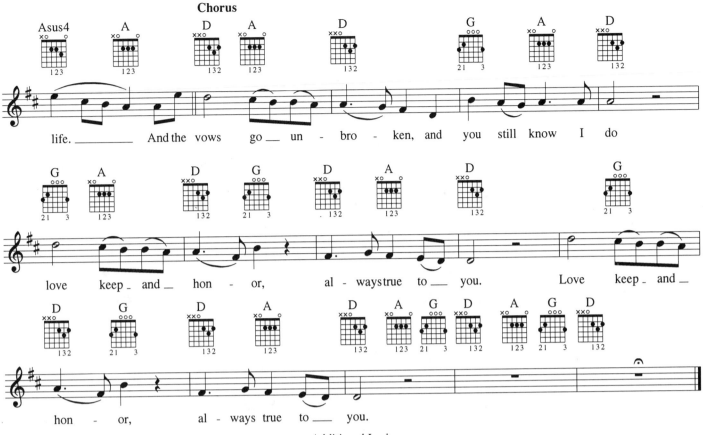

Chorus

life. _____ And the vows go un - bro - ken, and you still know I do

love keep _ and _ hon - or, al - ways true to _ you. Love keep _ and _

hon - or, al - ways true to _ you.

Additional Lyrics

2. And tonight when we kissed,
   You still took my breath away.
   It goes without saying,
   But I'll say it anyway.

3. Though I have been tempted,
   Though I have never strayed.
   I'd die before I'd damage
   This union we have made.

Your Cheatin' Heart

Words and Music by Hank Williams

Strum Pattern: 3
Pick Pattern: 3

Moderately Fast

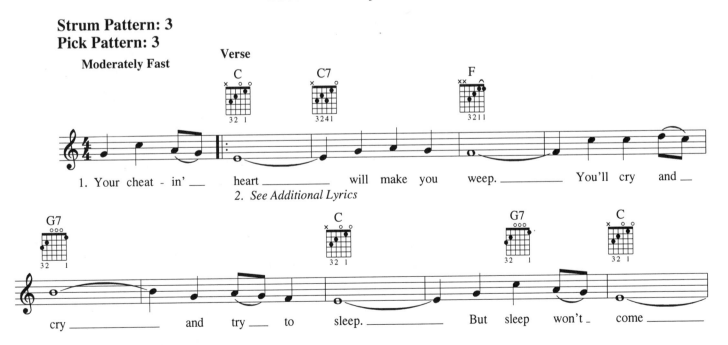

Verse

1. Your cheat - in' _____ heart _____ will make you weep. _____ You'll cry and _

2. See Additional Lyrics

cry _____ and try _ to sleep. _____ But sleep won't _ come _

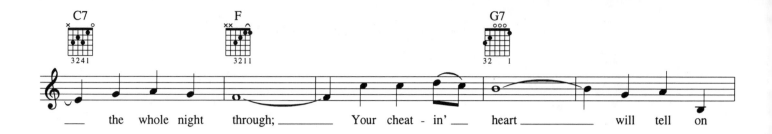

the whole night through; _____ Your cheat - in' ___ heart _____ will tell on

Bridge

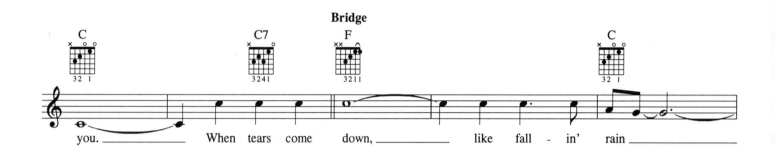

you. _____ When tears come down, _____ like fall - in' rain _____

___ you'll toss a - round _____ and call my name. _____ You'll walk the __

Chorus

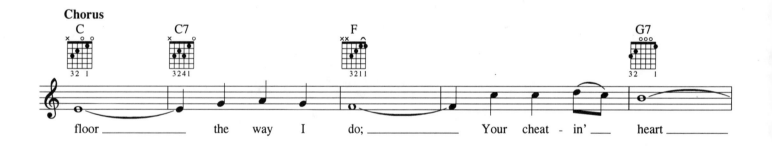

floor _____ the way I do; _____ Your cheat - in' ___ heart _____

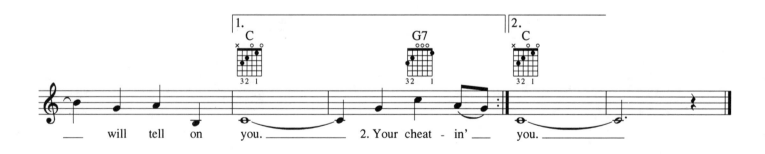

___ will tell on you. _____ 2. Your cheat - in' ___ you. _____

Additional Lyrics

2. Your cheatin' heart will pine someday and crave the love
   You threw away.
   The time will come when you'll be blue;
   Your cheatin' heart will tell on you.

154

Walking the Floor over You

Words and Music by Ernest Tubb

Strum Pattern: 3
Pick Pattern: 3

Additional Lyrics

2. Now, darling, you know I love you well,
   Love you more than I can ever tell.
   I thought that you wanted me and always would be mine,
   But you went and left me here with troubles on my mind.

3. Now, someday you may be lonesome too.
   Walking the floor is good for you.
   Just keep right on walking and it won't hurt you to cry.
   Remember that I love you and will the day I die.

Waterloo

Words and Music by John Loudermilk and Marijohn Wilkin

Strum Pattern: 3
Pick Pattern: 3

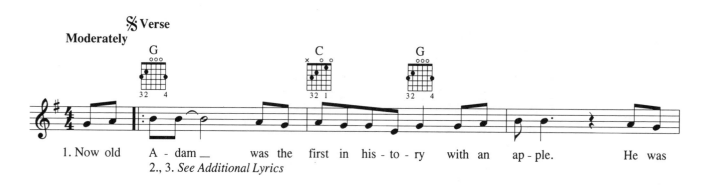

1. Now old A - dam _ was the first in his - to - ry with an ap - ple. He was
2., 3. *See Additional Lyrics*

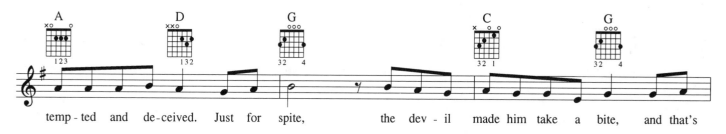

temp - ted and de - ceived. Just for spite, the dev - il made him take a bite, and that's

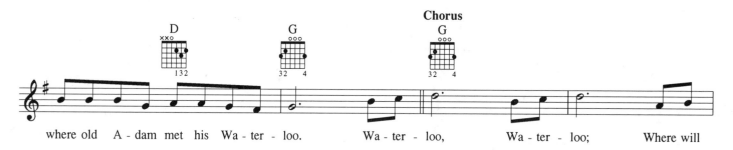

where old A - dam met his Wa - ter - loo. Wa - ter - loo, Wa - ter - loo; Where will

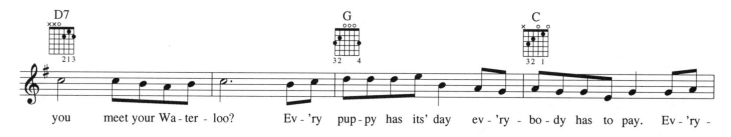

you meet your Wa - ter - loo? Ev - 'ry pup - py has its' day ev - 'ry - bo - dy has to pay. Ev - 'ry -

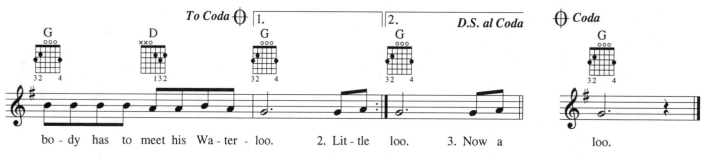

bo - dy has to meet his Wa - ter - loo. 2. Lit - tle loo. 3. Now a loo.

Additional Lyrics

2. Little General Napoleon of France
   Tried to conquer the world, but lost his chance.
   Met defeat known as Bonaparte's retreat.
   And that's where Napoleon met his Waterloo.

3. Now a fella who's darlin' proved untrue,
   Took her life, but he lost his too.
   Now he swings where the little birdies sing
   And that's where Tom Dooley met his Waterloo.

Welcome to My World

Words and Music by Ray Winkler and John Hathcock

When Two Worlds Collide

Words and Music by Roger Miller and Bill Anderson

Strum Pattern: 8
Pick Pattern: 8

Wheels

Words and Music by Dave Loggins

Strum Pattern: 1
Pick Pattern: 2

Intro
Lively

Verse

1. Some peo-ple are born to live a-lone _ and go a-bout life that ___ way. _
2. *See Additional Lyrics*

Their home _ is a long stretch of black-top, and ev-'ry day is just an-oth-er day. _

They like mov-in', stay-in' on the run _ and tryin' to make the world stand still.

Pre-Chorus

White lines _ and cit-y lim-it _ signs, and life is like an au-to-mo-bile ___

MCA music publishing

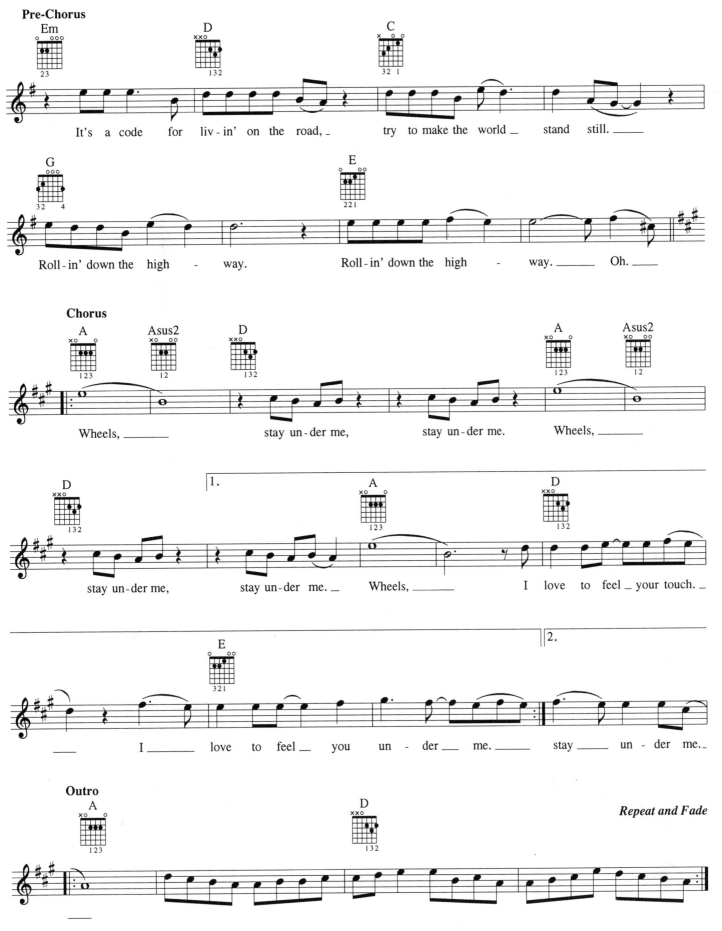

Additional Lyrics

2. It's a freedom that we all want to know and
   It's an obsession for some.
   To keep the world in your rear view mirror while you
   Try to run down the sun.
   It's a knowin' when you get where you're goin', you're
   Never there against your will.

Why Me?

(Why Me, Lord?)

Words and Music by Kris Kristofferson

Strum Pattern: 8
Pick Pattern: 8

Intro
Moderately

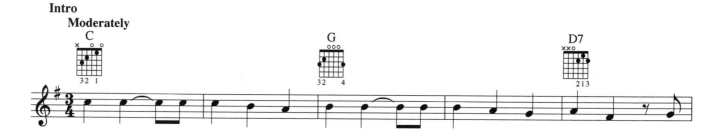

Verse

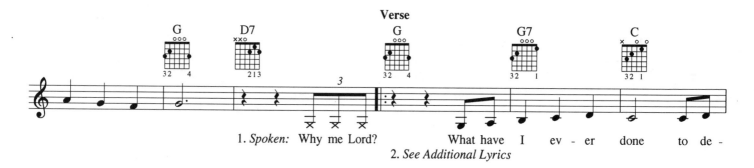

1. *Spoken:* Why me Lord? What have I ev-er done to de-
2. *See Additional Lyrics*

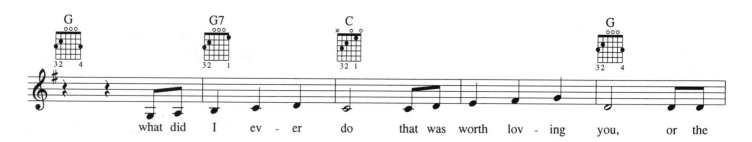

serve e-ven one of the plea-sures __ I've known? _____ *Spoken:* Tell me Lord,

what did I ev-er do that was worth lov-ing you, or the

𝄋 Chorus

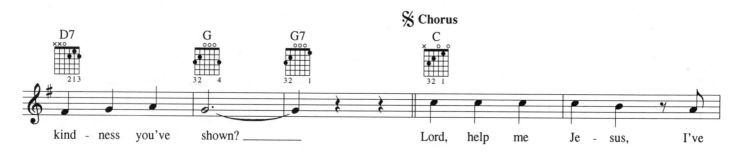

kind-ness you've shown? _____ Lord, help me Je-sus, I've

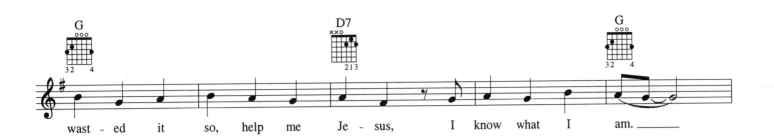

wast - ed it so, help me Je - sus, I know what I am. _____

But now that I know that I've need - ed you so, help me

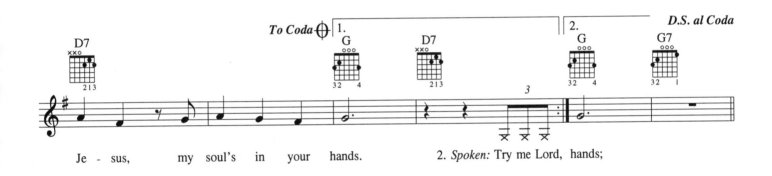

To Coda ⊕ | 1. | 2. | *D.S. al Coda*

Je - sus, my soul's in your hands.

2. *Spoken:* Try me Lord, hands;

⊕ *Coda*

hands. _____ Je - sus, my soul's in your hands. _____

Additional Lyrics

2. Try me, Lord, if you think there's a way
I can try to repay all I've taken from you.
Maybe Lord, I can show someone else
What I've been thru myself, on my way back to you.

You Decorated My Life

Words and Music by Debbie Hupp and Bob Morrison

Strum Pattern: 1
Pick Pattern: 2

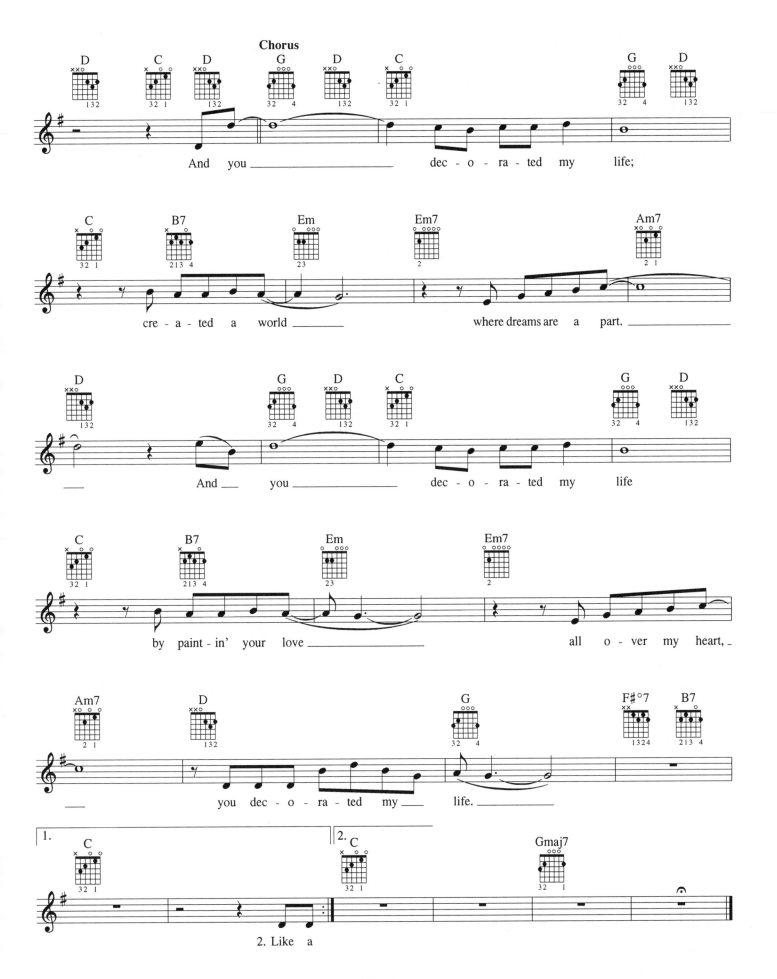

Additional Lyrics

2. Like a rhyme with no reason in an unfinished song,
There was no harmony life meant nothin' to me, until you came along.
And you brought out the colors, what a gentle surprise;
Now I'm able to see all the things life can be, shining soft in your eyes.

You Don't Know Me

Words and Music by Cindy Walker and Eddy Arnold

Strum Pattern: 4
Pick Pattern: 5

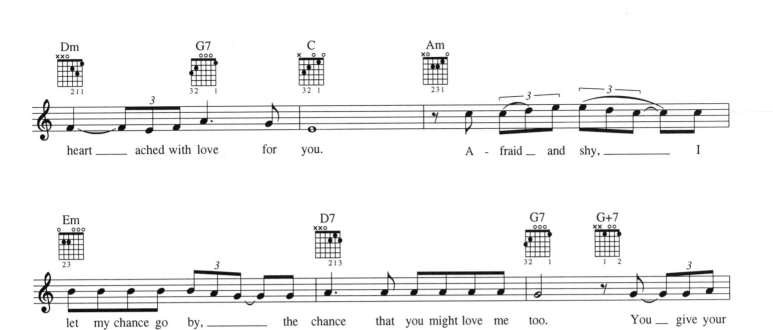

heart _____ ached with love   for you.   A - fraid _ and shy, _____   I

let my chance go by, _____   the chance   that you might love me   too.   You _ give your

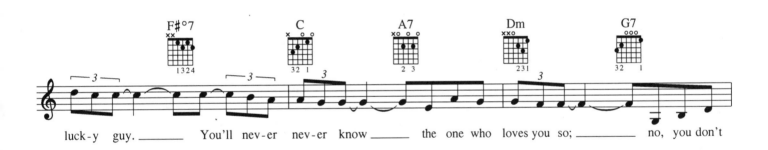

hand to me _____ and then you   say good - bye. ____   I watch you   walk a - way _____ be - side the

luck-y guy. _____   You'll nev - er nev - er know _____ the one who loves you so; _____ no, you don't

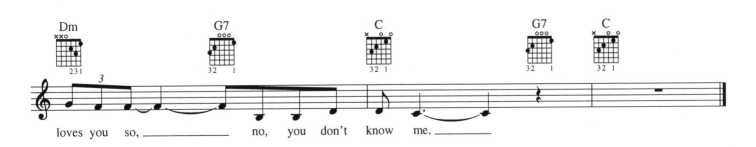

know me. _____   For know me. _____ You'll nev - er   nev - er know _____ the one who

loves you so, _____   no,   you   don't know me. _____

You Don't Want My Love

Words and Music by Roger Miller

Strum Pattern: 4
Pick Pattern: 5

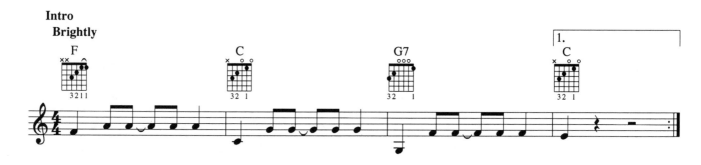

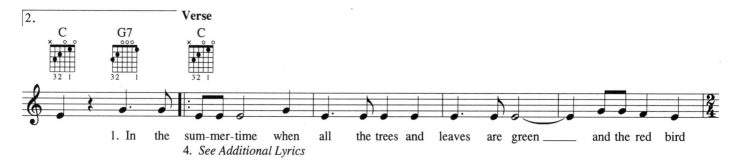

1. In the sum-mer-time when all the trees and leaves are green _____ and the red bird
4. *See Additional Lyrics*

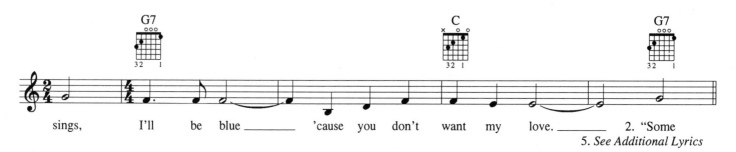

sings, I'll be blue _____ 'cause you don't want my love. _____ 2. "Some
5. *See Additional Lyrics*

oth - er time," that's what you say when I want you. _____ Then you laugh at me and

make me cry _____ 'cause you don't want my love. _____ You don't seem to care a

thing a-bout me, ___ you'd rath-er live with-out me than to have my arms a-round you when the

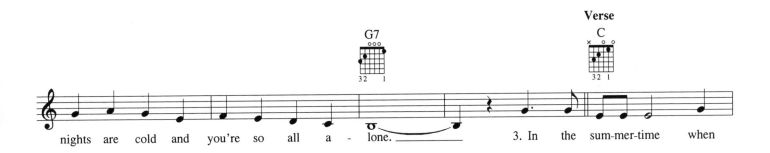

nights are cold and you're so all a - lone. ___ 3. In the sum-mer-time when

all the trees and leaves are green ___ and the red bird sings, I'll be blue ___

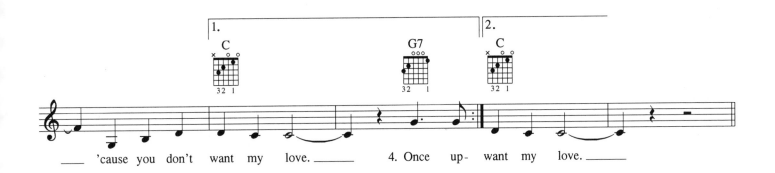

___ 'cause you don't want my love. ___ 4. Once up-   want my love. ___

Additional Lyrics

4. Once upon a time you used to smile and wave to me
   And walk with me but now you don't 'cause you don't want my love.

5. Some other guy is takin' up all your time.
   Now you don't have any time for me, 'cause you don't want my love.

You Needed Me

Words and Music by Randy Goodrum

Strum Pattern: 5
Pick Pattern: 2

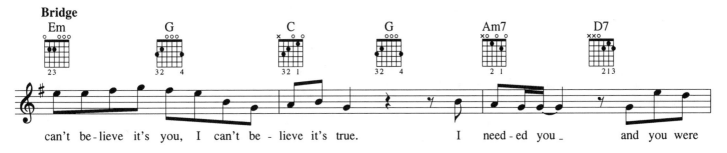

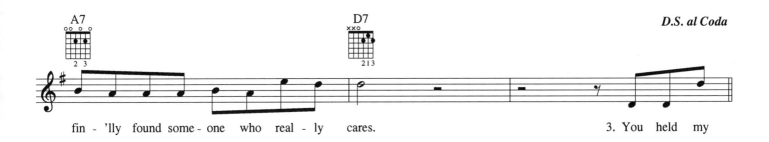

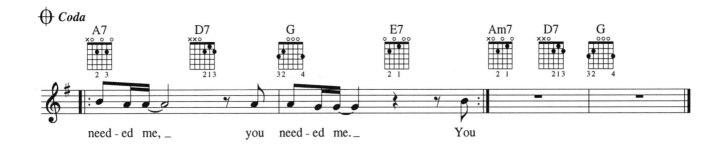

Additional Lyrics

3. You held my hand, when it was cold.
   When I was lost, you took me home.
   You gave me hope, when I was at the end,
   And turned my lies back into truth again.
   You even called me friend.

You're the Reason God Made Oklahoma

Words and Music by Sandy Pinkard, Larry Collins, Boudleaux Bryant and Felice Bryant

Strum Pattern: 1
Pick Pattern: 4

Additional Lyrics

3. Here, the city lights outshine the moon.
   I was just now thinking of you.
   Sometimes when the wind blows you can see the mountains
   And all the way to Malibu.

4. Ev'ryone's a star here in L.A. County.
   You ought to see the things that they do.
   All the cowboys down on the Sunset Strip
   Wish that they could be like you.
   The Santa Monica Freeway sometimes makes a country girl blue.

5. I worked ten hours on a John Deere tractor
   Just thinkin' of you all day.
   I've got a calico cat and a two room flat
   On a street in West L.A.

Will the Circle Be Unbroken

Words and Music by Eddy Arnold

Strum Pattern: 2
Pick Pattern: 2

Verse
Moderately Fast

1. There are loved ones ___ in the glo - ry ___ whose dear forms ___ you of - ten
2., 3. *See Additional Lyrics*

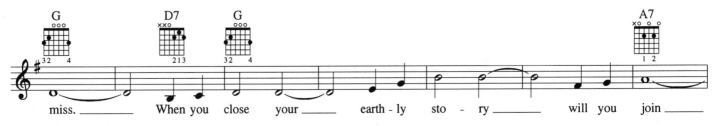

miss. ___ When you close your ___ earth - ly sto - ry ___ will you join ___

Chorus

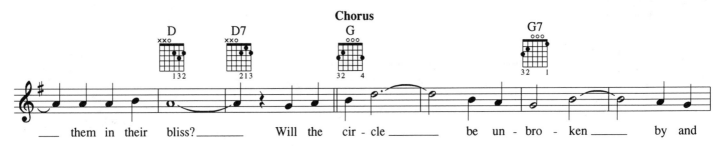

___ them in their bliss? ___ Will the cir - cle ___ be un - bro - ken ___ by and

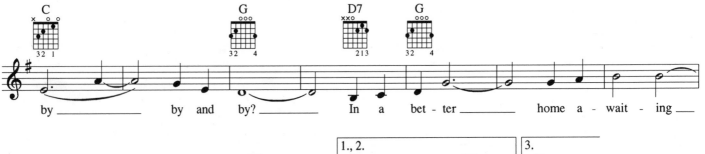

by ___ by and by? ___ In a bet - ter ___ home a - wait - ing ___

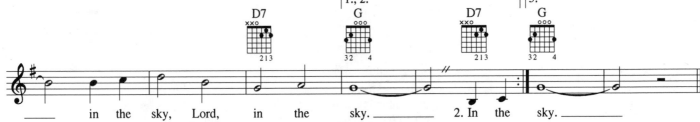

___ in the sky, Lord, in the sky. ___ 2. In the sky.

Additional Lyrics

2. In the joyous days of childhood oft' they told of wond'rous love.
   Pointed to the dying Savior, now they dwell with Him above.

3. You can picture happy gath'rings 'round the fireside long ago.
   And you think of tearful partings when they left you here below.

THE GUITAR TECHNIQUES SERIES

The series designed to get you started! Each book clearly presents essential concepts, highlighting specific elements of guitar playing and music theory. Most books include tablature and standard notation.

Acoustic Rock For Guitar

The acoustic guitar has found renewed popularity in contemporary rock. From ballads to metal, you'll find many artists adding that distinctive acoustic sound to their songs. This book demonstrates the elements of good acoustic guitar playing – both pick and fingerstyle – that are used in rock today. Topics include Chords and Variations, Strumming Styles, Picking Patterns, Scales and Runs, and much more.
00699327......................................$6.95

Basic Blues For Guitar

This book taps into the history of great blues guitarists like B.B. King and Muddy Waters. It teaches the guitarist blues accompaniments, bar chords and how to improvise leads.
00699008 ....$6.95

Music Theory For Guitar

Music theory is the cornerstone in understanding music. But how does a guitar player relate it to the guitar? This volume answers that question. Concepts of scale, harmony, chords, intervals and modes are presented in the context of applying them to the guitar. This book will open the door to not only understanding the fundamentals of music, but also the world of playing the guitar with more insight and intelligence.
00699329......................................$7.95

Finger Picks For Guitar

A convenient reference to 47 fingerstyle guitar accompaniment patterns for use with all types of music. In standard notation and tablature. Also includes playing tips.

00699125 ....$6.95

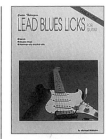

Lead Blues Licks

This book examines a number of blues licks in the styles of such greats as B.B. King, Albert King, Stevie Ray Vaughan, Eric Clapton, Chuck Berry, and more. Varying these licks and combining them with others can improve lead playing and can be used in rock styles as well as blues. Clearly written in notes and tab, you'll progress from the standard blues progression and blues scale to the various techniques of bending, fast pull offs and hammer-ons, double stops, and more.
00699325......................................$6.95

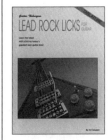

Lead Rock Licks For Guitar

Learn the latest hot licks played by great guitarists, including Jeff Beck, Neal Schon (of Journey), Andy Summers (Police), and Randy Rhoads (Ozzy Osbourne). The guitarist can use each lick in this book as building material to further create new and more exciting licks of their own.
00699007 ....$6.95

Rhythms For Blues For Guitar

This book brings to life everything you need to play blues rhythm patterns, in a quick, handy and easy-to-use book. Everything from basic blues progressions to turnarounds, including swing, shuffle, straight eighths rhythms, plus small, altered and sliding chord patterns. All are presented in the style of many of the great blues and rock blues legends. Includes notes and tab.
00699326......................................$6.95

Extended Scale Playing For Guitar

An innovative approach to expanding left hand technique by Joe Puma. The sliding first finger technique presented in this book will give players a new and broader outlook on the guitar. The book explores a variety of scales – major, minor, half-tone/whole-tone – and more.
00697237......................................$7.95

Right Hand Techniques

Through basic alternate, sweep and cross picking patterns, 10 chord arpeggios, palm muting and fingerstyle techniques, this book presents everything you need to know in getting started with the basic techniques needed to play every type of music. Additional topics include rhythm, rake and fingerstyle techniques. A real power packed technique book!
00699328......................................$6.95

Rock Chords For Guitar

Learn to play open-string, heavy metal power chords and bar chords with this book. This book introduces most of the chords needed to play today's rock 'n' roll. There are very clear fingering diagrams and chord frames on the top of each page. Empty staves at the bottom of each page allow the player to draw in his own chord patterns.
00689649 ....$6.95

Rock Scales For Guitar

This book contains all of the Rock, Blues, and Country scales employed in today's music. It shows the guitarist how scales are constructed and designed, how scales connect and relate to one another, how and where to use the scales they are learning, all of the possible scale forms for each different scale type, how to move each scale to new tonal areas and much, much more.
00699164 ....$6.95

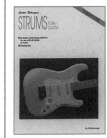

Strums For Guitar

A handy guide that features 48 guitar strumming patterns for use with all styles of music. Also includes playing tips.
00699135 ....$6.95

0495

WITH NOTES AND TAB

This series features simplified arrangements with notes, tab, chord charts, and strum and pick patterns.

The Best Of Aerosmith

20 of their hits, including: Dream On • Livin' On The Edge • Love In An Elevator • Sweet Emotion • Walk This Way • and more.
00702001 . . . . $12.95

The Big Christmas Collection

35 all-time favorites, including: Go Tell It On The Mountain • The Greatest Gift Of All • Happy Holiday • I'll Be Home For Christmas • Jingle-Bell Rock • The Most Wonderful Time Of The Year • O Holy Night • Silver And Gold • and more.
00698978 . . . . $14.95

Eric Clapton's Best

17 classics arranged for easy guitar, including: After Midnight • I Shot The Sheriff • Layla • White Room • Wonderful Tonight • and more.
00702090 . . . . $12.95

Eric Clapton – Unplugged

All 14 songs from his best-selling acoustic album, featuring: Hey Hey • Layla • Nobody Know You When You're Down And Out • Tears In Heaven • and more.
00702086 . . . . $10.95

Contemporary Christian Favorites

20 great easy guitar arrangements of contemporary Christian songs, including: El Shaddai • Friends • He Is Able • I Will Be Here • In The Name Of The Lord • Love In Any Language • Love Will Be Our Home • Say The Name • Thy Word • Via Dolorosa • and more.
00702006 . . . . $9.95

Contemporary Country Ballads

15 easy favorites, including: Fast Movin' Train • The Greatest Man I Ever Knew • I Never Knew Love • Rumor Has It • She Is His Only Need • Ghost In This House • and more.
00702091 . . . . $9.95

Contemporary Country Pickin'

21 easy country classics, including: Boot Scootin' Boogie • Chasin' That Neon Rainbow • Chattahoochee • Papa Loved Mama • Straight Tequila Night • and more.
00702089 . . . . $9.95

The Best Of Def Leppard

12 songs that even beginners can play! Songs include: Bringin' On The Heartbreak • Hysteria • Pour Some Sugar On Me • Photograph • Rock Of Ages • and more.
00702084 . . . . $12.95

Disney Movie Hits

10 fun favorites for beginning guitar players, including: Be Our Guest • Beauty And The Beast • Under The Sea • A Whole New World • and more.
00702085 . . . . $9.95

Gospel Favorites For Guitar

An amazing collection of 50 favorites, including: Amazing Grace • Did You Stop To Pray This Morning • He Lives • His Name Is Wonderful • How Great Thou Art • The King Is Coming • My God Is Real • Nearer, My God, To Thee • The Old Rugged Cross • Take My Hand, Precious Lord • Turn Your Radio On • Will The Circle Be Unbroken • and more.
00699374 . . . . $14.95

Guitar Wedding Collection

Over 50 contemporary sentimental favorites, including: All I Ask Of You • Dedicated To The One I Love • Don't Know Much • Grow Old With Me • Longer • My Funny Valentine • Somewhere Out There • Through The Years • Unchained Melody • When I'm Sixty-Four • and more!
00699394 . . . . $14.95

The New Best Of Billy Joel

15 songs, including: All About Soul • It's Still Rock And Roll To Me • Just The Way You Are • The River Of Dreams • Uptown Girl • We Didn't Start The Fire • and more.
00702087 . . . . $9.95

The New Best Of Elton John

17 of his best, including: Bennie And The Jets • Candle In The Wind • Don't Go Breaking My Heart • Goodbye Yellow Brick Road • Your Song • and more.
00702088 . . . . $9.95

Best Of Carole King For Easy Guitar

25 easy arrangements of her hits: I Feel The Earth Move • It's Too Late • (You Make Me Feel Like) A Natural Woman • Some Kind Of Wonderful • Up On The Roof • Will You Love Me Tomorrow • You Light Up My Life • and more.
00702011 . . . . $12.95

Rockin' Elvis For Easy Guitar

15 legendary hits, including: All Shook Up • Blue Suede Shoes • Don't Be Cruel • Hound Dog • Return To Sender • and more.
00702004 . . . . $9.95

The Best Of Queen For Guitar

19 simplified classics, including: Another One Bites The Dust • Bohemian Rhapsody • Crazy Little Thing Called Love • We Will Rock You • You're My Best Friend • and more.
00699415 . . . . $12.95

The Best Of The Rolling Stones

13 classics, including: Angie • Emotional Rescue • Hang Fire • It's Only Rock 'N' Roll • Start Me Up • Waiting On A Friend • and more.
00702092 . . . . $9.95

The Rolling Stones Collection

28 of their best, including: Angie • Beast Of Burden • Hang Fire • It's Only Rock 'N' Roll (But I Like It) • Start Me Up • Tumbling Dice • Waiting On A Friend • and more.
00702093 . . . . 17.95

FOR MORE INFORMATION, SEE YOUR LOCAL MUSIC DEALER, OR WRITE TO:

HAL•LEONARD™ CORPORATION
7777 W. BLUEMOUND RD. P.O. BOX 13819 MILWAUKEE, WI 53213